This book is a collaborative effort. Writers from all over the world submitted their work for consideration, with 68 stories being selected.

Publishing Syndicate strongly encourages you to submit your story for one of its many anthologies. You'll find information on how to do so at the end of this book, starting on page 316.

Dedication

To my wonderful grown-up kids Steve Ellsworth and Susan Rose for giving me the parenting practice that qualified me to create this book. And to my stepdaughter, Natica Gianunzio, who still, after all these years, calls me (fondly, I hope) "Wicked Stepmother."

To my parents, who did the best they could. The rest was up to us, their three children. Thanks for being there for us while we learned, grew and tested the limits.

Mom, thanks for encouraging me to write stories. And for teaching me the Palmer Method of penmanship. Even though you've been gone many years, whenever I see your beautiful handwriting, I hear your voice. What a great gift, the artistic gift of cursive writing that future generations will not know!

Dad, thanks for taking me fishing even though I tangled the line or snagged a tree every single time. I'll never forget the peaceful times on the sandy shores of the Columbia River, roasting hot dogs, drinking coffee from a Thermos, waiting for the bell on the fishing pole to ring and waving as the ships went by. Sometimes simple memories are the sweetest.

~~ Pat Nelson

Pat and Steve

Susan

Natica

Pat and her other kid, husband Bob

CONTENTS

4 Lost in Translation

5 Ready or Not!

6 You Just Never Know

7 All Grown Up

8 The Other Side of the Coin

Acknowledgments

We are thankful!

From Pat:

Thank you to my husband, Bob, for reading the first draft of my manuscript. It was a bit like having his help to change a baby. He read and suggested changes to "my third baby," the manuscript. Then he left me to clean up the mess. I also have to thank him for letting me talk to myself at my desk. He just smiled lovingly, as if I were an adorable baby babbling in a crib.

And thank you to Kathleene Baker, co-creator of *Not Your Mother's Book . . . On Dogs*, for being my cheerleader whenever I doubted myself. Huge thanks to the other NYMB co-creators, as well, who added encouragement and friendship. Because of this book, I now have a large circle of writer-friends in places I have yet to visit.

From Dahlynn and Ken:

Thank you to Dahlynn's teen son Shawn. Actually, Shawn should be thanking his mom for not sharing embarrassing stories about his childhood, even though step-dad Ken did sneak one funny story into the book.

And thank you to Shayla Seay for keeping the office running smoothly. We'd be up to our eyeballs in paper if she didn't keep nearly everything organized.

And from all of us at Publishing Syndicate:

A special thanks to the many writers who submitted stories for this book. You shared your parenting blunders, joys and nightmares. Without the things that went wrong, there would be no book and far fewer stories to make us laugh. We only wish we could have printed every story submitted. But keep submitting your stories for all of our new NYMB titles: www.PublishingSyndicate.com.

Introduction

*"A two-year-old is kind of like having a blender,
but you don't have a top for it."*

~~ Jerry Seinfeld

I could have chosen some deep, meaningful quote to introduce these stories, but the one above is more in the spirit of the *Not Your Mother's Book* series: silly, humorous and a little bit crazy.

Isn't that what parenting is much of the time? You're either laughing like mad or, by the end of the day, you're sure you've slipped over the edge. But once the kids have gone to sleep, once you've had a chance to regroup, you realize your children are your greatest blessings.

Parents aren't perfect. Never have been, never will be. There's only one time parents know everything, and that's *before* the kids are born. A mother myself, I can state that in spite of our imperfections, loving memories are born and raised, creating moments that later bring giggles, guffaws, hearty knee slaps and tears of laughter.

There are many great stories in this book, but fair warning: you might be a tad grossed out reading Chapter 2—"Stories That Stink." Hey, if you say you avoided those "natural disasters" of parenting, you're either lying or you had a live-in nanny! There are no exceptions when it comes to babies that pee, poop, pass gas or puke at the most inopportune times.

As children aim for adulthood, they are not the only ones who grow. Their parents must grow along with them. It's trial and error for both on this roller-coaster ride. Misunderstandings between parent and child create some of the most humorous memories and make for roll-on-the-floor-funny stories—but often not until some time has passed.

And why do the craziest, most embarrassing things with kids happen out in public, with an audience? Oh, sure, you love it when you can laugh at someone else's humorous parenting incidents, but what about when they involve *you* or *your kid*? That's another story, right?

Kids never mean to, but they all get into trouble. But even if you were fuming at the time, you have to admit some of those stories make good comedy material once the dust has settled. Seinfeld would agree: he has three kids and plenty of fodder for his stand-up acts!

Given enough time, kids grow up. Both parents and children have learned many lessons along the way. But when that time comes, the parents sometimes still try to raise their adult kids. Then eventually, the kids try to raise the parents, as in the story that concludes this book.

Parenting stories, whatever the age of the children or the parents, never cease to bring laughter—to those who are on the outside looking in or to those who take a glance backward. Have fun looking through this window at other people's parenting stories and laugh yourself silly reading this book.

CHAPTER
ONE

Baby Steps

Expect the unexpected . . .

Previews of Coming Contractions

by
Lisa Tognola

"Home delivery" used to mean a mustached man named Raul driving an oxidized Ford Pinto and tossing the morning newspaper into our neighbor's bushes. That was until my impatient third baby made a quick exit onto my living room floor and redefined the term.

It was 12:15 A.M. when I was jolted from my slumber by a drive to my gut with a 5-iron, followed by a series of wrenching contractions at five-minute intervals. This little baby meant business.

I felt as anxious as the day I found out I was pregnant with our first child, Heather. While my fellow graduate students awaited the results from their Experimental Psychology finals, I sweated out the results of my pregnancy exam at the student health clinic, the brightly colored condoms piled high on the counter, mocking me.

Now it was time for our third child to enter the world. "Honey, wake up—it's happening! I think I'm in full swing!"

I yelled to my husband, Chris, who lay as dormant as a bear in hibernation.

I repeated myself and gave him a nudge. He turned over and grumbled, "Keep your eye on the ball!" pulled up the covers and rolled back over.

Fighting rapid-fire contractions, I said, "Honey, I think I'm having the baby."

"Baby! Did you say baby?" Chris did a front round-off and vaulted from the bed like an Olympic gymnast.

"Start the car and call Mrs. Garner to stay with the kids!" I cried.

I tried to convince myself that this was a false labor, like the kind I once experienced when Chris and I abandoned a rack of lamb and carrots Vichy during a candlelight anniversary dinner at a five-star restaurant and headed straight to the hospital, only to return home to a reheated bowl of yesterday's chili over the 11 o'clock news. Maybe I was using avoidance due to the stressful conditions of Heather's birth, which took place at the end of the hallway in an overcrowded hospital bulging with women in labor, something to do with a full moon and Macy's annual sale.

But when embryonic fluid suddenly gushed out of me, I knew there was no denying it. I was glad Heather and our second child, Henry, were asleep in their upstairs bedrooms. This labor was real. In a panic, I waddled down the stairs and headed to the front stoop, where I collided with Mrs. Garner, our neighbor. "Where do you think you're going in this snowstorm? You get yourself right back into that house, young lady, or you'll have yourself a car delivery!"

"Yes, Mrs. Garner," I replied.

Did she say "car delivery?" I quickly wondered to myself. In my book, the only acceptable car delivery would be a newly purchased Baby Benz in my driveway. Yet I was terrified by the idea of having the baby at home.

I let Mrs. Garner guide me back into the house and into the kitchen. Uncertain as to how to proceed, I did what came naturally to me during times of stress—I reached for the cookie jar and groped my way to the bottom where I located one lone fortune cookie. I cracked it open and read the fortune: "All will go well with your new project." It should have read, "Car delivery today mean messy carpool tomorrow."

I pictured what the morning routine might look like: *Time to take Heather to school, kids. Get in the car.*

But Mom, there's a giant jellyfish on the floor!

Sweetie, that sea creature is just Mommy's placenta. Now step over the damn thing or we'll be late for school!

I moved into the living room to rest but found myself in too much pain to sit. By then, it felt like a team of Brazilian jiu-jitsu warriors were trying to fight their way out of my belly and I was beginning to think of childbirth less as a miracle and more as cruel and unusual punishment. I leaned forward, struck my best werewolf pose and let out a primal howl that rivaled the wild dogs in *Cujo*, the film based on Stephen King's horror thriller. Then I dropped down on all fours with my knees cushioned by our new living room carpet—the one that had led us on a three-year quest for the perfect-colored rug to match our gold and mauve living room.

A generally kind and gentle person, I ordinarily would

have welcomed Mrs. Garner's outreach of affection. But possessed with unworldly pain and glowing red eyes, I hissed, "Get your hands off me!" Mrs. Garner's arm recoiled from my flaming body. She may have wondered whether she needed to get help or garnish herself with a string of garlic.

The next thing I knew, my kids Heather, age five, and Henry, age two, were crying on the stair landing. Mrs. Garner ran upstairs to console them. *How have things strayed so far off course?* my brain questioned as I tried my best to keep from exploding, literally. The idea had been for her to watch our kids while I floated in anesthesia-induced bliss at the hospital.

"I don't want to have the baby at home!" I wailed. Nothing changed—until a moment later. I felt the baby's head and screamed, "I'm having the baby at home!"

"Everything's going to be OK," Chris assured me. "Let me give you a hug."

Or maybe it was, "Everything's going to be OK, just don't soil the rug." I don't quite remember.

As two policemen stormed through the door, followed by two volunteer emergency medical technicians, I regained hope. But I worried when the EMTs appeared to be younger than our high school baby sitter. I wondered whether they'd ever seen a vagina . . .

Within minutes of screaming to get the baby out of me, he glided out like a slippery bar of soap into the cradled hands of one of the EMTs. I heard, "It's a boy!"

Heather and Henry have a baby brother! In overwhelming relief, I responded, "Towels!"

Chris repeated, "Towels for the baby!" like a short-order cook.

"Towels for the rug!" I added. Then I provided detailed instructions to my husband on emergency carpet care.

As a group of men stood around my tethered baby scratching their heads, debating how to tie off the umbilical cord without a clamp, I watched Chris reach down to remove his shoelace. I reminded him of the recycling twine in the drawer next to the stove, and they used that, instead. Come to think of it, this was the first time we would use the twine for a special bundle, other than newspaper.

After arriving at the hospital, I was finally able to call my parents and congratulate them on the birth of their new grandson. Chris was proudly handing out "It's a Boy!" cigars when a nurse called him into the examining room. A few minutes later, Chris approached me, interrupting my conversation with my mom.

"Lisa, you're not going to believe this. We don't have a baby boy. It's a girl." I dropped the phone and stared at him. "The nurse said she looks beautiful. I peeked under the blanket, and she's right, it's a girl," he said, as he tenderly wiped a string of drool from my gaping mouth.

"Lisa, Lisa? Are you there?" I heard my mother's voice from the dangling receiver. I picked up the phone.

"Mom, scratch that. It turns out you have a granddaughter. Heather and Henry have a sister!"

"Lisa, did they give you drugs at the hospital?" she asked, trying to rationalize my gender confusion over my own child.

"No, Mom," I said as I spoke my thoughts out loud. "The baby must have been swollen when she was born and someone thought she was a boy."

"So what they saw wasn't a, a . . . " my mother asked

tentatively.

"No, Mom." With that, I hung up the phone.

The next day, my husband tried to convince me that it was the EMT who had called out our baby's mistaken gender, not him. It was then we heard the familiar sound of a dragging tailpipe that prompted my husband to go outside and retrieve the day's newspaper. This time, Raul's home delivery brought news of my home delivery. The local headline read, "New Baby Boy-Girl Born at Home."

Tognola kids

The Baby (Monitor) Blues

by

Ashley Jones

Nearly three weeks ago, something truly terrible happened.

The fabulous baby monitor that I have come to love stopped working. Now, I know what you're thinking—how hard could it be to replace a pair of white walkie-talkies? Well, this baby monitor is *not yo' mama's monitor*.

The choice of baby monitors nowadays is truly fantastic—digital video, anyone? It's mind boggling to buy anything for a child. Many mothers will sympathize.

The baby-gear market is a fascinating thing. When I was pregnant with my oldest child, Garrett, I walked into Babies "R" Us for the first time to register. I took one look at the entire wall devoted to pacifiers and bottles, started sobbing (yes, seriously) and walked right out. *How can one tiny person possibly need so much stuff?* I wondered. *How would I make the right choices?*

My husband, David, was more than willing to help me

register, but he quickly pointed out that if *I* didn't know what to get, *he* wouldn't know. In hindsight, I wonder if this was his way of avoiding the baby superstore. Well played, Mr. Jones.

Whenever I find myself in an unmanageable situation, I enlist the help of my mother. Overwhelmed by being a first-time mother, I explained to her that I could not face the task of registering alone, so she willingly joined me on the next trip. After seeing aisle after aisle of anything and everything your new baby could need, she agreed that visiting a baby superstore to register felt more like maneuvering a minefield. But ever the optimist, she assured me we would somehow plow through all of the baby items until we had registered for everything we actually needed. For one thing, we decided that yes, we needed the fantastic and amazing wipe warmer even though many people say it's a waste of money. And it's not! It's just not!

The problem with baby stores is the sheer amount of choices. There are at least 37 choices for each item! Don't believe me? Take a field trip to Babies "R" Us—I promise it will blow your mind. Along the way, Mom talked about what baby shopping was like in the good ol' days. Mothers would go buy the crib because there was only one choice. Similarly, mothers bought the highchair, the car seat and the stroller . . . because there was only one choice for each! What I wouldn't give to go back to simpler times.

Three hours later, we left the store exhausted, yet triumphant. We had finished! We had actually finished! Hooray for Mom!

As if you don't have to buy enough for your new bundle of joy, each choice comes with a subconscious message—and by that, I mean a completely conscious marketing ploy: "If you don't buy the very best, you are intentionally trying to harm your child," or "If you don't buy the top-of-the-line item, your child will grow up insecure and will undoubtedly turn into a dysfunctional adult." Sound dramatic? Tell that to the sales clerk who insisted, "The higher the coil count in a crib mattress, the better your child's physical strength and bone growth. You want the best for your child, don't you?" Sorry, lady, I will never pay $300 for a crib mattress. Never. I settled for the middle-of-the-line mattress and guess what? No skeletal deformities in either of my two children. So far, anyway.

As you can see, choosing things to buy for your baby is an often overwhelming task, so my current dilemma of having to research then go purchase a new baby monitor made me cringe.

So there I was . . . monitorless and unsure of what to do next. David and I decided our baby girl, Lyla, would sleep in our room again until we found a new monitor. The rule in our house is that a new baby can stay in our room until he or she is sleeping through the night, because who really wants to walk all the way across the house to soothe a crying baby at 3 A.M.? Not this girl! So after ousting Garrett from our bedroom at 10 weeks and Lyla at 12, I wasn't particularly thrilled for her to rejoin us at 16 weeks old.

Please don't misunderstand my need for a baby-less bedroom as cold or unloving. Honestly, I need a LOT of sleep myself, and all of the cute little noises babies make when they're asleep aren't so cute when they're keeping me awake. David, however, remains unaffected. He managed to sleep through me screaming during labor contractions at 2 A.M., so a few baby grunts and sighs are nothing to this guy.

The greatest digital video monitor ever made was a gift from a friend. And to be quite honest, it never really occurred to me what a baby monitor costs. When I was pregnant with Garrett, I knew this gift was coming, so Mom and I completely skipped the monitor aisle when we registered. In fact, Mom wasn't sure why I needed one.

"Do you really need a baby monitor?" she asked. "I never had one when you all were babies."

"But what if the baby cries?" I asked. "Wait, how did you hear me when I cried at night without a baby monitor?"

"We could hear you through the screen door if you needed us," explained Mom.

"The screen door? You used a screen door in place of a baby monitor?" I was shocked.

"No," Mom explained, "the screen door was there to keep the cats out. That way, we could still check on you without worrying about cats in the crib."

Wanting to do my homework, I researched new monitors online. I was hoping to find a decent video monitor for a decent price, but let me just tell you, $180 is NOT a decent price. That wasn't even the most expensive one. Ridiculous!

Being the money-conscious mama that I am, I looked at the basic audio monitors, but they just weren't the same. There's something fun about being able to watch your children on a little screen while they sleep or play in their rooms.

Realizing that a new video monitor was probably not in the family budget, I vowed to fix the broken monitor. I tried everything. I pressed each button . . . took the batteries out . . . put them back in . . . and tried a new wall plug. Nothing worked.

Heartbroken and no closer to a solution, I tabled the problem for two weeks. But this past Saturday, I decided I could no longer tolerate the precious nighttime baby noises. I started back at square one. I Googled. I eBayed. I Craigslisted. And I looked at every baby website ever created. Turns out, the video monitors were still expensive two weeks later. *Dang.*

So I vowed again to fix the broken monitor. I tried everything—again. Except . . . *Wait. What's that button? That button right there on the side of the camera? It must be new. It wasn't there two weeks ago when I tried everything to fix it the first time.*

Did you know that video monitors, like every other item that plugs in, have an on/off button? I discovered the camera was off. And the crazy thing is, when I turned it on, it worked!

I know what you're thinking to yourself: *Didn't Ashley go to college? Aren't people who go to college supposed to be at least somewhat smart?* Not only did I go to college, folks, but I have my master's degree. Good thing, too, because I almost spent $180 on a new monitor that I didn't need!

Finally, Lyla is now back in her room at night with a working monitor and I am again a happy, well-rested lady.

When I called Mom to tell her the conclusion of the baby monitor drama, she ever so optimistically said, "I actually think you're really smart. Most people would have bought a new one and probably wouldn't have been able to fix the old one like you did."

Thanks for the vote of confidence, Mom.

Lessons Learned from *Apollo 13*

by
Lisa McManus Lange

New mothers are often perceived as not knowing very much, and deep down, I was determined to prove those naysayers wrong. Even though I knew what to expect about the birthing process and the resulting little one, I also knew I still had a lot to learn. But my biggest lesson would be to follow my instincts—with the help of an astronaut.

It was the week before Christmas and I was already two weeks overdue. My doctor assured me Santa would not have to make a stop here in British Columbia, Canada, to deliver our baby. The baby would be born before Christmas. "Don't want the little one in the oven TOO long!" he joked with me.

This was the same doctor who had overseen my health since I was four years old, the same doctor who had delivered both my sisters. We had developed a comfortable relationship over the past 20 years; he understood my sense of humour and my way of thinking. As he guided me through my pregnancy, he never talked down to me, but with me. It was no surprise when one time, while listening to the baby's heartbeat on the fetal heart monitor, he compared the little life inside me to the movie *Apollo 13*.

"Think of your baby as a little being attached to the mother ship by a cord, floating around like the astronauts in *Apollo 13*," he said. I was tickled by his down-to-earth analogy, and giggled as I recounted his comparison to my husband.

Even though I had prepped, prepped and prepped some more, when my due date came and went, and two weeks had passed, bringing us closer to Christmas, I started to panic. What about my last-minute shopping?!

So my dear sister took me shopping, insisting on driving because of my delicate state. She even teased me that if she were to suddenly slam on the brakes of the car, she could get my labour to start. She, too, was anxious.

People in the stores veered around me, and I had fun telling people I was two weeks overdue. Their apprehensive looks as they assessed me head to toe—as if they were expecting to see a puddle of water suddenly appear underneath me—only encouraged me to reveal my overdue, delicate condition even more. I wasn't too worried, as the next day, I had another visit with my friend—the doctor.

I went home to my husband only, ironically, to watch the movie *Apollo 13* starring Tom Hanks. The Christmas tree was up, all my last-minute errands were done, and all I could do was watch the movie and wait. We were at the part when Tom Hanks had just missed his chance to land on the moon, his instincts telling him to turn his broken spaceship around and head home to earth, when the first pain hit. Then another. Then another.

I did as previously instructed and called the hospital. Despite being two weeks late, I got the proverbial pat on the head from the nurse on the phone. "Don't worry, dear, this is your first baby, there are always false alarms . . . " She thought of me as a first-time mom who knew nothing. "Come in if you want," she said. "Things are slow in labour and delivery tonight. Babies must be holding out to be New Year's babies!"

So off we went, excited and nervous, while the nurse called my doctor.

At the hospital, I was met with condescending, knowing smirks, the kind new moms get when they panic over every little thing. They *temporarily* admitted me and said to wait for the doctor, who was attending the doctors' annual Christmas party.

Not a moment too soon, the doctor arrived—but in a suit. A suit to deliver my baby, I tell you! The first thing I blurted out was, "Don't you think you should change? You're gonna get a bit dirty." My labour pains had calmed down a bit and my sense of humour hadn't left me—yet.

After a quick exam, the doctor told me to stay at the hospital, but then half-heartedly mumbled, "It might be a while yet."

Not 45 minutes later my son was born. Luckily, my doctor's instincts matched mine. He had delayed heading home and chatted with others at the nurses' station, at least until several nurses from my room rushed out to grab him. I barely made it up onto the bed when in strode my doctor—in scrubs, not in his suit—just in time to deliver my son.

If I hadn't listened to my instincts, my baby might have

been born in front of the TV, with Tom Hanks watching in the background. I guess even as a first-time mother, I knew a few things after all!

Oh, and I didn't name my son Apollo, either.

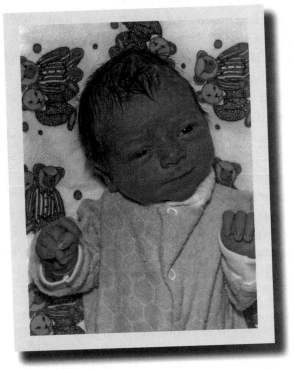

Newborn Mitchell Lange

Hooked Up

by
Erika Hoffman

"That's disgusting!" shrieked my 20-year-old daughter Heather as she scowled at the breast-feeding mother at the table across from us. Christmas music, the clatter of plates and the jocular exchanges of spirited diners bounced off the walls in the banquet room.

"What did you say?" asked my 88-year-old father, leaning toward his granddaughter. Heather rolled her eyes to the ceiling, crossed her arms and grunted. "Papa, don't look at the table across from Mom! That woman's nursing her newborn right here in the middle of Maggiano's while we're trying to digest calamari!"

"Oh?" Dad swiveled his head around immediately to witness the partially exposed woman. He shrugged and turned toward me. "Is it unusually loud in here?"

"It's Christmas week; folks are celebrating," I explained to my old man.

"Did I order yet?" He knit his brows.

"Veal parmesan. Remember?"

He shook his head. "I don't remember things too well."

"Oh, brother," groaned my daughter, glaring at the new mom. Heather let out a turbo sigh. The nursing mother left the table across from us and ambled toward the booth behind us to join her party.

"Yuck! Unbelievable! She's walking with the baby attached to her teat!" My daughter emitted a gagging noise. The woman slid in behind me. Her proximity ensured her hearing the comments of my vexed offspring. The infant squalled in my ear.

"How obnoxious!" my daughter exclaimed. Without acknowledging the brouhaha, the young mom placed her child in a stroller and pushed him back and forth in the narrow aisle as the harried waiters pulled in their guts to squeeze by.

I didn't know which was more annoying—the shrieking infant or my daughter's self-righteous attitude. We'd only been served our salads, and I prayed our main courses would materialize soon to take my daughter's mind off the infant. A gush of laughter peeled from the gang behind us. The baby matched it with an earth-shattering, wall-bouncing, echo-making scream. I almost joined in.

"You'd think she'd be courteous enough to take her howling brat outside," Heather bleakly announced.

The mom picked up her tot and soon he started suckling and slurping again. My daughter let loose an agitated sigh. Her disapproval was palpable. The mom detached the babe, returned him to his stroller and made a hasty retreat to the restaurant's atrium.

"Thank goodness!" declared Heather. "It is abominably rude to nurse in a crowded restaurant where diners are enjoying the Christmas holiday. Who'd do such a thing?" she pontificated. She looked me in the eye. "Mom, what do you think of public breast-feeding?"

Trying to avoid answering my daughter's question, I searched around eagerly for the waiter. I saw him approaching with our entrees. He placed Dad's gargantuan portion in front of him.

My daughter continued her line of questioning after all the entrees had arrived. "Mom, you nursed us, right?"

"Uh-huh," I murmured with my mouth full.

"You never breast-fed in public?" persisted Heather.

"My veal tastes like chicken," I commented, realizing, as I took a bite of my food, that I had been served the incorrect entrée. But my goal was to change the subject.

My daughter glanced over. Realizing they brought me the wrong order, she snapped her fingers in the waiter's direction.

"Really, it's OK. It's tasty," I hastily replied.

"He'd better adjust the bill." She stuck out her chin assertively. "I just can't believe the waiters didn't say anything to that mama. How rude to hook her kid up to her nipple here in the midst of us all. I even saw a peak of pink areola."

"Where is this woman?" asked my dad, suddenly curious about the peak of areola.

"Grandpa, you don't want to see that!"

"Speak for yourself," he answered wryly.

I peered over at my indignant daughter. I smiled wanly.

"Heather, when I was your age, I thought like you. I regarded that part of my anatomy as decorative rather than functional. Then I had children. When your brother or you were hungry, I became oblivious to everybody and everything except your little groping mouths."

My daughter made a lemon face. "Yuck, that's gross! You're making me lose my appetite."

"Honey, your day will come. When you become a frazzled mama with a crying kid, you won't be so critical."

Heather waved her fork, tines pushing out toward me. "Nope! Not me! That's what bottles and husbands are for."

"That's what I said, too, when I was 20!" I laughed. I waved my fork back at her. "Just you wait. And quit bothering the nice waiter. My chicken's delicious."

Double the Fun

by
Pam Bostwick

I struggled onto a city bus with a heavy diaper bag, a white cane, one twin in a front pack and the other in a stroller. The bus was crowded. I am legally blind, yet could see enough to tell there wasn't an empty seat. My hearing aids squealed with the noise around me.

"Hurry up, lady!" the bus driver yelled at me.

"You can have my seat," a woman said.

Relieved, I sat down. "Thank you." I turned down my hearing aids and settled the babies on my lap.

The woman spoke again. "They're precious. What a handful, but twice the happiness."

"Yes," I said, smiling. She didn't even know about my other five children!

Someone got off the bus, so the woman sat down by me. I threw a blanket over my shoulder to nurse one baby while jostling the other. The woman cooed at him and he cooed back.

"You handle two babies like a pro."

"That's nice of you to say." I was hanging on for the ride of my life. "I'm glad it's no more than two babies at a time."

She chuckled and we lapsed into thoughtful silence.

I readied the babies, and then heard the bus driver say, "3500 S. Redwood Road."

That was my stop, so I exited the bus. I waited at the curb until the traffic to the right of me moved. Then, with my little bit of sight, I saw the cars in front of me stop for the red light. I crossed the street. As I walked the few blocks home, my mind drifted back to where it had all started.

"Twins!" I had shrieked in the examination room. My yelling must have reached the waiting room, for in seconds my friend Elaine burst through the door.

"What's going on back here?" she asked.

Then I heard her say, "Wow! What a blessed day!" She explained to me later that the nurse had put up two fingers.

I felt miserable in the Utah summer. I was so big that someone could roll me down the street, which would have been easier than my waddling along. The doctor said I needed to go to bed the last two months to keep the twins from coming early. Fat chance of that with grade schoolers *and* teens demanding my attention!

Then someone played a prank on our family by shredding newspaper all over our yard and lathering shaving cream on the trampoline. My kids pitched in to clean up the mess. My belly flopped and bounced as I crawled and felt around on the ground, picking up debris. I had already been using my stomach as a table for my plate of food.

I couldn't touch my toes to cut my toenails or get comfortable when I lay down. Elaine walked with me around the block every day to keep my morale up since my tired uterus only dilated one centimeter a week.

Near the end, low blood sugar made me sick and I couldn't eat. I stayed up ill one entire night, pacing and pleading, "Oh, my babies, please hurry up and come."

I checked into the hospital early in the morning. The nurse gave me an IV for dehydration. This relaxed me and I went into labor. The babies came quickly without medication and with my family watching. When each baby crowned, everyone cheered and one of my daughters exclaimed, "Our little buddies are here!"

Amazed and exhausted, I held my first twin, Jacob, close. I gently touched his face and each tiny toe and finger to make sure he was perfect. Suddenly I wondered, *Where's my other baby?* That's when I heard the doctor say, "We saved another one."

My son Jarom had to stay in ICU because the umbilical cord had wrapped around his neck and he suffered with my low-blood-sugar problem. I wept all night without Jarom. "All I want to do is hold him. I almost lost him," I whispered to the nurse. As soon as Jarom miraculously stabilized in the morning, I clung to him. I was able to bring both boys home after two days.

Taking care of two babies wore all of us out. Double the feeding—I felt like a Jersey cow! But breast-feeding beat hassling with bottles. It helped me bond with my babies, and it was easier for me, being blind. Double the diaper changing!

I could afford disposables, so I didn't stick myself with pins. I don't think I slept or showered for a year.

After the boys had been home a week, a friend stopped by to visit. "I'm curious about something. How do you tell the boys apart if you can't see their features?"

"Oh, that's easy," I explained. "Jacob has hair and Jarom doesn't." They are fraternal, not identical twins, and as they grew older, people told me they hardly resembled brothers. One had blond hair and the other brown. I treated them as individuals. I didn't dress the boys alike except when they were babies, and once as twin girls on Halloween. They never forgave me for that one! Even though they were only three years old at the time, family members keep that memory alive.

Each boy has a unique personality, and each one chose his own kind of mischief. Jacob, husky and active, dumped out sugar, put peanut butter sandwiches in the VCR and plugged up the toilet with his underwear. Meanwhile, Jarom, who was wiry and small, crawled into the oddest places and I spent hours looking for him. Someone suggested, "Why don't you put bells on their toes so you'll know where they are?"

"That wouldn't do me any good," I replied. "Due to surrounding distractions, I can't hear the bells, even with hearing aids."

"How do you keep track of them, then, with your disabilities?"

I shrugged. "I suppose by the grace of God and mothering intuition."

I had my quiet time while the older kids went to school and the twin boys took naps. During these rare moments, I breathed deeply and listened to the crickets and birds, sounds I could hear in the silence with hearing aids. When the twins woke up, I reveled in their cute chatter, even though I couldn't distinguish all of their words. My visual loss kept me from seeing their faces clearly, but I touched their cheeks and enjoyed their giggles.

Raising twins is truly an adventure. I like to say the twins are double the adventure, double the joys, double the love for two little boys. But the family had a saying while the twins were in the terrible-two stage: "They're double the trouble, double the fun, *double the work* for everyone!"

Jarom and Jacob

The Rocky Road of Parenthood

by
T'Mara Goodsell

As I stood at the end of a long grocery store checkout line filled with harried holiday shoppers, my water broke. From that point on, nothing would be the way I had meticulously planned my first delivery.

Maybe things had gone awry even before that day. I had, after all, wanted to have a March baby, so knowing it took an average of three months to conceive, I went off birth control in March. My reproductive system obviously didn't believe in the law of averages, and I got pregnant right away. My March baby was going to be a Christmas baby. Hence, here I was going into labor just days before my due date, right in the middle of the holidays.

My doctor being away for the holidays wasn't part of the plan, either. I cried while I signed the cesarean section consent form, protesting that I did too have strength to keep pushing—but they kept telling me I'd be glad I had the surgery. I never was. Of course I was eternally grateful that the baby was healthy, but this unfamiliar doctor's desire to go home and celebrate just didn't seem like a good reason to go through major surgery or the horrendous recovery that followed.

Colic definitely was not a part of the plan, either. I was going to take such good care of my baby that he would have no need to cry. I would be rested because I would simply do as my doctor suggested and nap when the baby slept.

But this baby screamed, purple-faced, every day and night, no matter what I did. And he dozed for no more than 20 minutes at a time—in between bouts of crying, of course—so that he'd wake up just about the time I'd relaxed enough to nod off. The few times I did fall asleep quickly enough, salespeople called and woke us all again. Did I need portraits? Life insurance? Educational baby toys? I didn't know it was possible to feel so exhausted.

And things continued to get worse. My father had a heart attack followed by open-heart surgery. The dog developed bladder stones and had to have surgery, leaving us both miserable and limping through puddles of dog urine all over the house. I even slipped on the stairs while carrying the baby. I instinctively held onto the child instead of the railing and landed in a sitting position. My son was fine, but I had shattered my tailbone and could barely walk.

One day, I called a child-abuse hotline. "I think I've abused my baby," I cried. The calm voice on the other end asked me what I had done. "I swore!" My baby was a perfectly clean slate, and I had ruined him. I, an avowed non-swearer, had used a curse word in front of a two-month-old infant. I feared my child would grow up to be a trashy, horrible, foul-mouthed person, and when people asked him where he had learned such words, he would say, "My mom taught me every- thing I know."

The kindly woman on the other end explained that, while it wasn't particularly good to swear in front of a baby, if that was all I had done it would probably be OK. "Babies don't give a lot back at first," she explained. "Just wait, he will."

Slowly, the baby stopped crying quite so much. One day, he smiled at me. I burst into tears and danced with him around the room, while the nearly recovered dog wagged his tail and joined in the fun.

One day while the baby cried and the dog barked to go out, the phone rang—just as the dishwasher began to smoke. I picked up the phone to what I assumed was more salespeople and shrieked, "I can't talk now—the dishwasher is on fire!" It turned out to be the pediatrician's office confirming an ap- pointment. I hung up the phone feeling like a fool. I dislodged the baby-bottle part that was caught in the dishwasher's heat- ing coil, and then opened windows to air out the smoke.

And then, something snapped. Or maybe it clicked. I thought, *Could it possibly get any worse? Yes! Yes it could!* I re- alized that we were alive, after all. The house hadn't burned down. The pain of the surgery decreased a little each day. The baby was alive, and aside from the colic, he was healthy and growing like a weed. My father had lived through his heart at- tack and surgery and was on the mend. The dog was alive and getting happier by the day as he healed, too.

To my surprise, I went from crying to giggling like a maniac. We were alive! We were surviving this craziness, and damn it—sorry, baby, I mean, darn it—we would continue! I wasn't responsible for the insanity in my life. I couldn't change it, couldn't control it. But that was OK. All I really needed to do was continue to survive it.

I suddenly realized for the first time the lesson I so desperately needed to learn: my son was not mine. He belonged only to himself—to his own agenda—and parenthood wasn't about planning his life or controlling the events surrounding it. A parent is only a guide. All I could do was step back and respond with as much love as I could muster.

It was then I surrendered, in a good way. I got a quart of rocky road ice cream from the freezer, slumped against the wall and slid to the floor (into a kneel so as to protect my tailbone), laughing like a fool with my beloved dog on one side of me and my wonderful, colicky baby on the other. I shared tiny licks of ice cream with the baby and the nuts with the dog—and ate the chocolate chunks myself. There we sat, the three of us, united over ice cream. It was no longer them against me, but all of us, together, taking on this great adventure called life.

Baby and dog

The "Baby" Bottle

by
Virginia Funk

"What do you mean you're ovulating and you want me to come home?" my husband querulously asked me over the phone. "I'm up to my ears in work. I have to get this paperwork done. Yes, I know we have to grab the opportunity when it arises. I'll try to get home early."

This was just one of the many conversations my husband and I had when we planned to start a family, but Mother Nature had other ideas. I just couldn't get pregnant. We watched the calendar for the favorable day called *ovulation*, and hoped we got it right. Needless to say, romance went out the window. For instance, how romantic is it when you have to carry your husband's sperm in a little bottle so the doctor can check it? In order to keep the bottle warm, the doctor said I should put it in my brassiere and drop it off at his office. Boy, that was a fun day. Can you picture going to the desk and reaching into your décolletage, pulling out a bottle of sperm, and presenting it to the nurse?

However embarrassing, I would have stood on my head to become a parent. The day finally came, and our son was born. My husband presented me with an orchid when he picked me up from the hospital. With our tight budget, it was comparable to Queen Elizabeth's announcement of the birth of Prince Charles. The newsreels showed her waving from the balcony of the palace. I, too, stepped out onto our fifth floor balcony and waved to my friends. Our apartment overlooked the parking lot. Mine was a royal birth, too. After all, my brothers sometimes told me I acted as if I thought I was a princess.

In the intervening years, it occurred to me that we weren't taught about how to be parents. We just flew by the seat of our pants. Dr. Spock was my mentor. His book became so dog-eared that I had to buy a second copy.

It was hard to get advice from my mother because she lived 500 miles away. Trying to get my questions answered in a brief one-minute, long-distance conversation was challenging. Long distance calls were for emergencies only because of the cost. My Italian mother nervously said in the middle of our short conversations, "This is costing you money, sweetheart. Goodbye." Then she promptly hung up before my questions were answered.

A baby sister followed two years later, and then the parenting really began in earnest. I turned everything into a lesson for the children. When my son was around five, he came in from playing in the cornfield next to the house. We lived in a farming community. "Mom, I saw a lady and a man. They came on a motorcycle, and they went into the cornfield, took off all their clothes and started wrestling."

Explaining that situation took a lot of parenting skill. I figured it was a tad early to teach him about the birds and bees, so I told him since it was an awfully hot day, the reason they undressed was to cool off. Then I lectured it was improper to take off one's clothes outside. But I wondered—could it be that they were desperately trying to conceive and that the time was right?

Our children are now grown and married with children of their own and they are good, decent, loving people. I like to think we succeeded in our job as parents. I would have had more children if Mother Nature had cooperated, even if it would have meant carrying more bottles of sperm in my brassiere.

Field Notes from the Playroom Floor

by

David Carkeet

The sonogram was murky, but there could be no mistake—my wife was carrying twins. While she seized my hand and struggled to come to terms with this kink in nature, I, a linguist, stared at the screen with a single thought: *Research opportunity!* Linguists had studied their own singletons, but none had studied their own twins. I would be the first!

I read *A First Language.* I read *Language Development.* I read *Conversations with a One-Year-Old.* I sent off to the NEH, NIH and NSF for grant applications. I foresaw funding and acclaim for something I would be doing anyway—hanging out with the kids.

But in Anne's and Laurie's first year, I learned that I could not be both father and observer. I would like to say that I threw my notebook aside and declared, "By God, I'm going to enjoy these babies." The truth is I spaced out. My analytical self took a holiday. I understand now what happened. Childcare requires a mental fleeing of the scene on a regular basis. I've seen it in playgroups, in preschools and even at the zoo. Next time you're there, watch how a mother chimp's eyes glaze over. She knows she's in it for the long haul.

My written record from those days, alternately detailed and gap-riddled, proclaims ambivalence. Unfinished sentences suggest that Dad, on the verge of a breakthrough, opted instead to take a nap. But I managed to stay awake for a few landmarks, like the girls' identical first word—"ball"—followed immediately by "bye-bye." I noted that gestures usually accompanied both words—a ball thrust forward, a squeezed wave. Once, at the end of a large family picnic, as the farewells were flying, 14-month-old Laurie worked her hand privately at her side, feverishly squeezing with every "bye bye" she heard, even though most of them had nothing to do with her.

And I have this happy documentation of a milestone achieved by 20-month-old Anne: "A. last night produced 1st 2-wd. sentence. She was putting on wool hat, taking it off, etc. I was lying on floor looking up at her, she looked down, eyes suddenly glimmering, & said, *dada ah* ('Daddy's hat'), whereupon she instantly tried to put the hat on me. Very exciting." And very odd, I now think, that I could seriously write "whereupon" in these notes.

Although I moved on to other projects, I continued to track the girls' linguistic progress, and 13 years later, that of their little sister Molly. The single most important thing I have learned is that children will do their own thing, on their own schedule, and they will defy efforts to correct them.

Every child modifies adult words to suit his or her

nervous system, musculature, and—it sometimes seems—whim. Among the near misses in our house were the twins' "bapo" for "apple" and their names for each other, "Nana" and "Lala," all pronunciations illustrating how toddlers favor consonant plus vowel syllables. The modifications can go much further, though. In *Growing Up with Language*, Naomi Baron describes a child in his second year who handled long words with a rule as ingenious as Pig Latin: he combined the first consonant with the final vowel. His word-cruncher turned "tomato" into "toe," "honey" into "he," and "monkey" into "me." To a parent encountering operations like these, it's as if the child is following an imp's language manual—a grammar written by Pippi Longstocking.

At the age of three, our youngest daughter, Molly, invented a beautiful general rule that produced these phenomena with machine-like precision: "bemember" for "remember," "Pebecca" for "Rebecca," and "pabella" for "umbrella." The rule modified the adult target word by inserting a "b" or "p" if the word began with an unaccented first syllable. It also produced "pomato" for "tomato," which makes me wish I could have gotten her together with the kid whose first-consonant-plus-last-vowel rule turned "tomato" into "toe." I imagine Molly saying, "It's not *toe*, you nincompoop. It's *pomato*!"

Children's independence extends beyond pronunciation into grammar. The daughter of a friend of mine went through a stage of saying "box-ox" as the plural of "box." Where could she have gotten the idea to do this? The answer is from her brain, from the innate equipment that allows children to interpret the data flying at them—equipment that readies the child for any language, not just English. Repeating part of a word for plurality is in fact a process that exists in other natural languages. Some languages even repeat the whole word: in Malay, kapal means "ship," while kapalkapal means "ships." The girl had a reasonable theory for making plurals, but she just applied it to the wrong language.

Anne and Laurie likewise charted their own grammatical course before joining the adult mainstream. Like many toddlers, they learned the object form of pronouns first ("him") and used it for all purposes. They said "him go" long before they said "he goes." If I said, "That's his car," they agreed with a firm "That him car." Their reanalysis of adult data was so aggressive that in their pronunciation of the word "history" they operated on the "his" that they somehow discovered within it and produced "himstory." The word "history" isn't ordinarily part of a preschooler's lexicon, and I wasn't reading Winston Churchill to them. It was Christmastime, and they were singing of Rudolph's future fame: "You'll go down in himstory."

When the girls sang those words, all I could do was stare at them in wonder. I certainly didn't correct them. They were like young scientists momentarily working with the wrong hypothesis, and eventually they would find the right one. Besides, correction would have had no effect. For years, both girls said "upside over" for "upside down," even when I repeatedly prompted them with an exact model. "Say 'upside down,' girls."

"Upside over!"

One incident demonstrates Anne's and Laurie's incorrigibility so strongly that I didn't need to record it in writing. It happened during a family visit with the girls' great aunt Cora.

A chain-smoking, retired career army nurse, Cora had no children of her own and therefore was a child-rearing expert. Shortly after our arrival, it became clear that Cora was not pleased with the way these two girls, at age four, pronounced "s." Their rule for making a word like "cups" was "cup" plus floppy wet lip noises; "desks" was a deluge. Cora sat them down on the couch and lectured them, making them say "s" over and over. "Say it," she said, pointing a bony finger at them. "Say 's.' Say 's.'" The girls, earnest pupils, dutifully filled the air with their spray.

What were the fruits of this instruction? Certainly not any change in their pronunciation. But there was an effect, of sorts. I eavesdropped on the girls later during the visit, when they were alone in a bedroom, playing with their dolls. For this particular drama they had given one of the dolls—the villain—a new name. They called her "The 'S' Lady."

The Carkeet twins

The Modest Mom

by
Dawn Caunce

I was so excited. The mailman had finally delivered my new breast-feeding apron. Oh, to be able to feed in public without fear!

The last straw had come Tuesday at playgroup. That's what we call play dates here in England. After what seemed like ages of feeding my little guzzler, who proceeded to let out a deliciously satisfied burp, I wrestled with the obscure clasps that some man must have invented, and may have exposed myself a little too much. At least that's what my friend said.

Anyway, my new apron—or shall I say "deluxe breast-feeding apparatus"—was gorgeous. Well, almost. I asked Mum to get me one for my birthday. There was one on the website that I had drooled over. She bought me the one shown next to it, the brown one instead of the pink one. She never listened to instructions.

I ripped open the packaging rather too childlike. I couldn't help it—it felt like Christmas. It was brown with swirly red bits on it and, well, huge. Practical, I suppose. Following the instructions and "placing it carefully over the care giver's head," thoughts of suffocation and baby came to the forefront of my mind. So, there I stood, modeling the apron. I bobbed Ben back and forth while showing my husband, Geoff, how marvelous my new fashion accessory would be and the difference it would make.

All my supportive husband could say was, "Hmmm, looks a bit like a butcher's apron." Great, knock a girl's confidence. I wished Mum had listened. The pretty French rose one would have been so much nicer. *Maybe I'll just use this one at home*, I thought. I lifted Ben, and he spat up all over the new apron— more washing! I wondered if everyone washed the same amount as me. I could take out shares in Whirlpool.

I still have yet to use the apron in public—if I ever do— especially after last week's fiasco when Uncle Tom and Glenda came over to our home for a visit. I probably did look foolish fumbling around while trying to feed my son, with his baby legs poking out from underneath the brown fabric. But the baby had to eat. And Geoff said I should just be confident when I fed our child and not worry about others.

I would love to have seen him get *his* bits out in public, or in front of relatives as was the case this evening, especially if they resembled crusty shriveled prunes like mine. I thought half my problem was that I still had to use the nipple shields, you know, those contraptions new mothers sometimes use to help their baby latch on. But I wondered why they weren't sticky—mine kept falling off. And Uncle Tom's face? It almost fell off, too, as he took a bite of the lovingly home-baked cake as he watched Ben's head bob up and down under the apron. The poor baby was only rooting desperately for his lunch.

With all this attention from our company, the butcher's apron, which seemed huge at first, now felt small. Then to make matters worse, a shield full of milk dropped to the floor and milk splashed in every direction, just missing Uncle Tom's plate. With the shield now on the floor, I offered my son a swollen crusty prune, but for some reason, he favored the smooth silicone feel of the teat. He protested.

Geoff eyeballed me, so me being me, I eyeballed him back.

"What?" I said, flinging my hands in the air just as Ben decided to bob his head up, exposing my left breast for everyone to see. I grabbed what fabric I could. Uncle Tom, sitting in the chair next to me, blushed profusely. Glenda, bless her, tried to distract everyone with tales of the Women's Club and how one of the women had brought vodka-filled soda bottles to the meeting.

"Do you think you would be better in the bedroom, dear?" Geoff asked as he ushered me upstairs to sit on my own for the next hour while I fed the baby.

Ah, privacy. There was no need for the apron now, so I whipped out my engorged breast. That felt good and Ben seemed to agree, snuggling up close, relishing the skin-to-skin contact. Placing the breast-feeding pillow and cushions on either side, we settled in for the feed.

"Dawn! We're going now . . . "

What time is it? Oh no . . . I must have dozed off. Guests! No! I have guests! Damn! I'd better not appear rude. Being careful not to wake Ben, who snored away in my arms, I laid him down gently in the Moses basket and tiptoed as quickly as I could out of the room.

Rubbing the sleep out of my eyes, I stood at the top of the stairs. Uncle Tom, Glenda and Geoff stood at the front door gawping up at me.

"Sorry," I said with a big goofy smile, "must have dozed off." *Jeez, was there any need to stare at me like that?*

Geoff eyeballed me again.

"What?" I mouthed. However, he was doing this strange wide-eyed manic look, nodding his head in an even weirder fashion.

"What?" I shrugged my shoulders, fed up with all the strangeness coming from Geoff. Ben began to scream.

That sudden familiar needle pain hit my nipple. *Thank God I have my breast-feeding pads on. Oh my . . . my pad . . . my breast!* I clutched my naked breast that lolled out of my top. As I stood on the top of the stairs with my boob out, tears suddenly welled in my eyes. Ben, even from the bedroom, picked up my distress and began to wail louder. Unfortunately, this set a sudden spray of milk squirting in all directions—my "let down" really hadn't let me down as it fired all over the ceiling and stairs.

Unable to move, I just stood there. I wanted the ground to open up. *How will I ever be able to face them again?* Tears pricking, I was immediately embarrassed and felt sorry for myself. Then I could not hold it in any longer, and I started laughing. I belly-laughed so hard it hurt. The three joined me; Geoff howled and Uncle Tom roared and Glenda kept repeating, "Stop it, don't,

I'm gonna . . . " while holding onto the banister cross-legged.

I never wore the apron again after that. I had somehow forgotten that breast-feeding is a natural and timeless gift and that as mothers, we have the God-given right to feed our children and that there is no need for contrived modesty. The apron is up to $5 on eBay right now.

Dawn and baby, sans apron

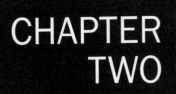

Stories that
Stink

Surviving the natural disasters of parenthood.

Potty Mouth

by
Karen Mykietka

I'm thankful that our oldest child is no longer in diapers, because traveling with a potty-trained toddler can be a challenge.

The three of us—my husband, our two-and-a-half-year-old son and I—were returning home after a family trip to the Canadian portion of the Rocky Mountains. Just 15 minutes after our supper stop, our son announced he needed to go pee. Luckily, we were just on the outskirts of Calgary, Alberta, so we exited the highway and searched for a suitable place to stop. Spotting a restaurant, we pulled in and took him into the bathroom, making sure to purchase some coffee to show our appreciation for his using the facilities.

About 20 minutes later, from the back seat of the van, we heard, "I need to go poop."

"What? You just went to the bathroom!" I responded, sipping my coffee.

By now we were on the open highway with no bathroom in sight. I thought back to when he had his last BM and realized it had been at least 36—if not 48—hours. So he likely really needed to go. From his car seat, he moaned and whimpered, "Need to poop."

Finally, we spotted a small gas station and pulled over. My husband jumped out, unbuckled him and the two rushed in. Less than a minute later, he ran back with our son, who was now crying.

"What's wrong?" I asked them both.

"The owner said they are closed and won't let us in to use the bathroom."

How ignorant! I thought. We reassured our little guy we would find another bathroom in a few minutes.

We sped down the road to a small town a few kilometers away and screeched to a halt in a restaurant parking lot. When my husband returned to the van, he said our son only went *number one* again. I knew our toddler's pleas for a bathroom would start the minute we hit the highway. So I took this opportunity to give him a snack, hoping he would relax and that the food would stimulate his need to go.

A little later, I decided I would give my husband a break and took our son into the restaurant's bathroom. He sat on the toilet and for 15 minutes, he went . . . and he went . . . and he went! During that time, and as he sat on the toilet, he chattered away nonstop. I was privy, quite literally, to a running commentary on his bodily functions.

"Me making a big poop."

"Are you all done now?"

"No, me need to fart and make more poop."

I commented that it stunk.

He responded, "Turn the fan on."

"It's already on," I said.

"The fan take my stinkies away?"

"Yes, it will." I had explained the function of the bathroom fan to him a few days earlier.

Someone entered the stall next to us.

"Someone in that toilet?"

"Yes."

"That another little boy?"

"No, it's a lady."

"What that lady doing?"

"She's going to the bathroom."

We heard the flow of urine. "The lady make pee."

Chuckling, I responded, "Yes."

"The lady have a vagina?"

I tried not to burst out laughing. "Yes, she does."

"You have a vagina, Mommy?"

"Yes, I do."

"You laughing, Mommy."

"Yes. You're a very funny boy."

"No, you a silly mommy."

Finally, he was done. I helped him off the toilet and he commented on the size of his poop. At least this time he didn't launch into a descriptive of his poop being a snake or a train. He flushed the toilet and asked as he pointed to the floor, "Where the poop go? Poop go there?"

I had corrected him last time when he thought it went up

into the tank of the toilet. "The poop goes out to the sewage plant where they clean the water," I replied.

We returned to the van, where his father waited for us. As I strapped our little guy into his car seat, he made a big announcement. Looking proudly at his father, he said, "I made a big poop and it went out to be cleaned."

Cole

Cheese Cutting 101

by
Kathryn Cureton

I live in a house full of men—a husband and two teenage boys. I have abandoned any hope of bonding through teddy-bear tea parties on the front lawn, Barbie fashion shows or impromptu mane-styling sessions with My Little Pony.

The nearest I've come to such tame activities was the time my youngest son accidently received a My Little Pony toy in a Happy Meal. From other past tear-filled experiences, I knew to order the meal with a boy's toy, but I forgot to check the bag before we drove away. It wasn't long before the error was brought to my attention by the nine-year-old. "You got me a *girl* toy! That's not fair!" He threw the toy on the floor of the car. "I'm not touching it!"

His brother, then 12 years old, picked it up. "This is cool. It's a merry-go-round. I'll show you how it works." It wasn't so much that he was interested in the toy, but rather that he saw a way to get into my good graces while making his brother mad.

We don't call him "Genius" for nothing.

The toy was great fun. The fact that it was pink did nothing to deter Genius from his mission. "Look, Mom. It goes around and around." At home, he and I had a rousing good time with it for about 30 minutes. Then it broke. But not before we coined a new name for his little brother: "The Pony."

My boys enjoy most things mechanical, such as rubber-band guns that launch tiny plastic pigs, as well as insect robots and remote-control battering rams. It came as no surprise when they pooled their pocket money for a rocket toy that changed citric acid to hydrogen fuel. It seemed like a reasonable purchase. After all, it had to be safer than the contraption their dad made for them that involved the water hose, two-liter soda bottles and an industrial air compressor.

That evening, as I stood at the kitchen counter hacking a 16-ounce hunk of cheddar cheese into smaller portions—or "cutting the cheese," as my boys prefer to call it—I heard a noise. It came from the front of the house: *Pfffffitttt*. It sounded like the noise a toy rocket that runs on water and citric-acid-made hydrogen might make as it shoots into the air and sprays chemicals on my kids. The kitchen overlooks the backyard, so I couldn't see what the boys were doing. I hollered for Genius, the idea being that if he didn't answer, he was out front launching his rocket. I was quite surprised when he responded.

"Yeah?"

"I thought I just heard you out front launching your rocket. It was loud!"

The boy answered from the direction of the bathroom.

"No, that was just me. I farted."

I heard The Pony laughing from his bedroom, which is next to the bathroom. Not that the situation itself was something he found funny. He was accumulating blackmail material. "You'd better not tease me at school, or I'll tell your friends the rocket story!" It was a sort of Cold War scenario. One boy didn't want anybody to know about the My Little Pony toy, and the other didn't want them to know that his fart was mistaken for a rocket launch. An uneasy truce was declared—one that is still in effect today.

The next week, the boys had a day off from school. They set about the business of honoring their unspoken pact, which was an ongoing plan to drive me crazy that day. It started that morning with a sound—a sound very much like that of a rocket launching in the front yard or a 12-year-old boy farting on the toilet. I heard it in my basement office. The Pony had his own desk in there and was playing *Civilization 3* on his computer. I turned to him. "Did you hear that?"

"Genius has launched another rocket," he said, eyes never leaving the monitor.

A fart of such magnitude seemed impossible. From the sound, I imagined Genius would be wildly flying around the room, just like a rapidly deflating balloon. It was that forceful. I hollered upstairs, "What are you doing?"

Genius laughed an evil laugh. The next thing I knew, he was standing right behind me. And I heard it again. The rocket-like rumble. The evil laugh. I told him he was nasty and to get away from me, right now, this very instant, or I was taking away his laptop for the rest of the day. Genius continued to laugh.

Then the boy spilled his little secret. "Mom! I wasn't really farting. Look. I have this straw down my sleeve. I blow in it and it makes my armpit sound like a fart! Listen. *Brraaapppp!* See? And it's not really a fart, just air in my armpit. You lean down like you're tying your shoe, make the fake fart, and then you hide the straw like this. I learned it at school yesterday when the boy who was born in a truck did it with a piece of an ink pen. We all thought it was a fart. He showed us how to do it. Isn't it cool?"

"Yes," I mumbled over my shoulder. "That's very cool. I'm so glad you're learning something at school." His fake-farting prowess validated, Genius ran off with his fart straw to attain perfection, like a magician logging mirror hours with a rabbit and a hat.

Genius practiced his newfound skill until I called the boys for lunch. As I scooped a grilled cheese sandwich out of the skillet and poured more milk into a bowl of Circus O's, The Pony began to taunt Genius and his fart straw, grabbing at the contraption.

"Mo-om! The Pony won't let go of the end of my fart straw! It's plugged up! I can't fart! Make him stop it. Now!"

The Pony giggled a fiendish giggle, fueled by the sugary Circus O's. He did not let go of the fart straw, despite being told twice.

I had finally had enough. "STOP PLUGGING YOUR BROTHER'S FART HOLE!" I yelled at my younger son.

Both boys stopped their scuffling and looked at me, mouths agape. "Wow! I bet that's something you never thought you'd be saying to your kids, huh, Mom?" Genius was always good at seeing the big picture. He turned to his brother and giggled. The Pony snorted. Genius dug a straw out of the drawer for The Pony. The fart-straw master and his new apprentice forgot their feud and hurried away to polish their act before their father got home. Never underestimate the power of a fake fart in brotherly bonding.

All of you mothers of daughters can go back to putting the finishing touches on your Easter bonnets. Bake a batch of cupcakes with rainbow sprinkles. Dash off a fan letter on butterfly-and-unicorn stationery requesting an autographed picture of Justin Bieber.

You really don't know what you're missing.

Genius (Jesse)

The Pony (William)

Hanging 'Round the Men's Room

by
Norine Dworkin-McDaniel

"NO, MOMMY!" My preschooler had dug in his heels and was refusing to budge. "I can't go in *there*!"

We'd just pulled off the turnpike into a gas station/convenience store because I really had to pee. The "there" into which I was trying to coax—OK, drag—my son, and rather quite unsuccessfully, was the Women's Room. My shifting from foot to foot, with thighs clenched tight, was hardly what you'd call negotiating from a position of strength. I wasn't about to leave him outside alone and was desperate to get him to go in there with me.

"*Maaaah-meeee*," my boy protested, exasperated.

"What is it?" I demanded, trying to tug him forward and vowing to myself that I'd be more diligent about doing my daily Kegel exercises from then on.

"I can't go in there," he protested, eyeing me as if I were quite possibly the densest adult he'd encountered in all of his four-plus, world-weary years. "I'M . . . A . . . BOY!"

Of course, the gaping hole in his logic—if boys can't go into the girls' bathroom, I couldn't very well go into the boys' bathroom either—escaped him. But before I could lay out that counter argument, he'd wriggled free and darted into the Men's Room, forcing me to follow him into what turned out to thankfully be a spacious single-seater. Apart from the urinal and the male pictogram on the door, the Men's Room was identical to the Women's Room that he'd steadfastly refused to enter.

It's times like these when I'm reminded that parenthood isn't a sprint. It's not even a marathon. It's a frickin' Iron Man crossed with an Iditarod. Just when you think you've cleared every possible hurdle in the particular parenting endurance test known as Potty Training, you run smack into yet another wholly unforeseen obstacle: the preschooler's stark understanding of gender identity as it pertains to the loo: boys go in the Boys' Room, not in the Girls' Room.

Though a discussion of gender fluidity is no doubt beyond his tender years, I had thought we'd gotten past those workaday bathroom hassles once the kid mastered the fine art of depositing his bodily wastes into the bowl. A challenge, I might add, that required the patience of 10 Dalai Lamas, not to mention the ability to suppress my gag reflex and *ewwww!* response. Like when I caught my son rolling poop pellets over the carpet as if they were marbles. Or when I had to actually sit down on a public restroom floor and patiently wait to see if he'd do more than just swing his legs and sing while perched on the toilet after shouting at me, "GO POTTY!" in a crowded restaurant. He didn't. And no, there isn't enough Clorox to get over that. Ditto for when I had to explain why to him it was unnecessary to strip off all his clothes when using a public bathroom, and how it was equally unnecessary to sit his bare bottom down on that same public restroom floor to put his clothes back on again. Yes, just thinking about it still makes me queasy.

Along the way, my preschooler had some setbacks, like when he figured out how to out-game our reward system— a Hot Wheels car for every successful potty experience. He did so by dropping a pellet at a time into the bowl then demanding a toy car for each and every effort. Or when we were out to dinner with my in-laws and I boasted that we were "D-O-N-E" with potty training. My son hadn't worn a diaper in weeks and my words still hung in the air between us when, as he sat on my lap, he wet his pants, soaking both of us. I ended up blow-drying my pee-soaked khakis in the pizza joint's ladies' room.

But yes, once my son had so thoroughly demonstrated his potty prowess that I finally stopped packing his in-case-of-accident clothes every time we left the house, I figured the days of bathroom challenges were behind us. What I hadn't expected was the push-back over location, location, *location*, as my son's desire for greater independence met a budding sense of gender identity.

Don't get me wrong. It's not that I'm squeamish about using the Men's Room. If a restaurant has single-person bathrooms marked "W" and "M" and the "W" is occupied, I'll tell any guy who thinks he can duck in front of me just because

"M" opens up first that he can wait his turn. When lines at the Ladies' have been exceptionally long, I've boldly stridden into a sparsely populated men's room with a full tank of liquid courage—and consequently, a full bladder—locked myself in a stall and went about my business. I figure I don't have anything that a man hasn't seen by the time he's reached, say, 25 (hopefully many times over). Still, I can hardly hover over a dawdling preschooler while other gents queue up at the urinals, right? Besides, while I want to encourage my kid's can-do attitude, who lets a four-year-old scamper, unsupervised, into a strange lavatory? That's like begging for legal commentary on the *Nancy Grace* television show.

Still, shit—uh, poop—happens, as I discovered on a recent layover at Cleveland Hopkins International Airport. I'd sent my cherub into an airport men's room to join his father only to discover—when repeated calls to him brought no reply—that my husband had actually gone into *another* lavatory farther down the concourse. That meant my baby was in a strange men's room all by himself. If that brings to mind every twisted *Law & Order: Special Victims Unit* episode ever produced, trust me—I've already experienced the nightmares. So, I recruited some wingmen.

These days, when my oft-traveling husband's not around to do the honors, my nephews, my brother-in-law and my father good-naturedly step up so that the youngest member of our brood can *pish* with the big boys. And when it's just he and I? Well, let's just say that old habits die hard. If the lad sprints for the stalls, you'll probably catch me going in after him. Men, be forewarned!

Norine's little pisher!

The Family Photo

by
Shari Courter

I should preface this story with the fact that my husband has always hated family photo day. It's not that I loved it, but it was important to me. We used to have photos professionally taken, made into Christmas cards and sent out the day after Thanksgiving. Notice the past tense? Let me tell you what happened in 2002.

Zac was eight, Aubrey, six and Kearstin, three. We also had two adorable black Labs. What could be more precious than including our dogs in one of our Christmas photos? I scheduled a pet-friendly session at a studio just 15 minutes from our house. What could go wrong?

Well, where do I begin? Right off the bat, two major mistakes were made by both my husband and me that played a huge part in the scenario that followed:

1. We had chili the night before and I made the unfortunate decision to give the leftovers to the dogs.

2. He fed the kids chocolate donuts for breakfast before we left.

Bear with me. This will all make sense in just a second.

After breakfast, we got dressed up in our holiday photo clothes and everyone looked nice. Anyone who knows our family would agree with me when I state this is unusual for us. We never get dressed up and although I hope we look nice when we go out, that's not the objective. Our main goal is for everyone to be fully clothed, a lesson we learned that very same year when all five of us managed to get from our house to our van then to a church softball game without anyone realizing that our youngest daughter was naked from the waist down. But I digress.

On this particular day, our neighbors got the rare treat of seeing us all in clothes as we loaded into the van. But it wasn't long before things took a downhill slide. We had barely made it onto the highway when we noticed the effects of the leftover chili on our dogs. In almost slow motion, the smell permeated each of our noses, and everyone's eyes opened to their fullest capacity. I jerked my head around to check Kearstin, who has the most sensitive gag reflex of us all. She was sitting in her car seat, violently dry heaving. Before the dry heaves could become wet heaves, I started promising her things if she didn't vomit. "If you don't throw up, I'll give you balloons and candy when we get to the mall!"

If you approach parenting the way I do, with the knowledge and acceptance that your kids are going to end up in therapy anyway, you will have a lot more freedom in the things you're willing to say in any given circumstance. Thus, my promise of balloons and candy seemed to do the trick, until the next round of silent, but deadly, gas escaped from the dogs. Without drawing attention to it, my husband tried to subtly deal with the situation by activating all of the automatic windows. Wind began whipping through the van—and our hair. But that's neither here nor there.

The problem with that idea, besides the destroyed photo-day hair, was that his action managed to spread the smell faster. This time no balloon in the world was able to stop Kearstin's regurgitated chocolate donuts from appearing down the front of her beautiful Christmas dress.

I suppose now is a good time to tell you that Aubrey has the second most sensitive gag reflex of our family and I have the third. Not only did the dogs continue their gassy antics that had started this debacle in the first place, but it turned into "Puke-Fest 2002." Our minivan-turned-wind-tunnel flew down the interstate as my husband yelled loudly, "Everyone stop vomiting right now!"

For future reference, ordering someone to stop vomiting has a zero success rate.

Zac, who inherited his dad's nonexistent gag reflex, began removing Kearstin's filthy dress while my husband did a U-turn. We arrived back in our driveway a mere 15 minutes after we left. Unfortunately, those same neighbors who experienced the rare treat of seeing us all dressed up as we climbed into our van earlier were still outside to witness our car squeal into our driveway. Two smelly dogs and four wind-blown, chocolate-puke-covered people poured out of every available door, followed by a now-naked Kearstin who happily skipped into the house, eagerly asking when she was going to receive her balloons and candy.

I wouldn't expect a Christmas photo from us any time in the near future, if I were you.

Kearstin and one of the fart dogs

Oh Shucks, It's Just Oysters

by
Kimberly McRaney-Blake

One summer, my family and I went camping along the Oregon Coast. We loaded up the minivan, grabbed the kids' favorite uncle and his girlfriend and set out for one of the state parks that dotted the coastline.

After unloading and setting up camp, the kids were starving. We decided to head into town to find some seafood. Being near the ocean always intensifies our seafood cravings. We ended up at a little seafood stand that, along with a seafood market, also included hot food.

We each ordered. Our youngest son, Nick, who was five, decided to try fried oysters for the first time. He has always been adventurous when it comes to food. After eating about three-fourths of his serving, I noticed the oysters were not fully cooked. It didn't bother Nick at all, and because people eat oysters raw all the time, I figured it would be OK.

While we were eating, my parents surprised us by calling

to say they had come to the beach to stay a few nights. They no longer camped, so they had checked into a hotel several miles up the road. The kids were thrilled to learn that Grandpa and Grandma's hotel had an indoor swimming pool. First thing after breakfast the next morning, we packed our suits and headed to the hotel to swim while we waited for the sun to come out and heat up the sand at the beach. The boys happily played in the pool with their dad while their uncle and his friend enjoyed the nearby hot tub. With the boys entertained, I had the wonderful opportunity to sit poolside and visit with my parents.

About 20 minutes into our swimming adventure, my son secluded himself in a corner of the pool and became very quiet. This was unusual for him. I got up from my chair and walked over to him to see what was going on. As I approached, I noticed several little black chunks in the bottom of the pool. When I reached my son, I bent down and asked him, "What's wrong, Nick?"

He stated, with some reluctance, that he had gotten rid of his bad oysters. Not wanting to embarrass him, I quietly told him, "It's OK, oysters happen. Get out of the pool so Mom can help you clean up."

I tried to act nonchalant as I walked over to my older son and told him, "Get out of the pool. We have to go, now." He jumped right out.

As he treaded water, my husband saw the boys climbing out of the pool. He looked up at me and asked what the matter was. I explained to him that our son had pooped in the pool, due to the bad oysters he had eaten the day before. He became appalled over my news and scurried out, grabbed a handful of towels and jumped back into the shallow end to try to clean up the mess.

This, for some strange reason, seemed funny to the kids' uncle. He sat in the hot tub laughing. He even sang a song about the predicament, one I can't repeat here.

Meanwhile, my husband continued reaching underwater with the pool towels, fishing for the dreaded "oysters." Even though he was red in the face—from the effort and the embarrassment—he was doing a great job of not calling attention to himself. That was, until a man swimming toward him from the deep end of the pool stood up and stepped on one of the oysters that rested on the pool's bottom. The man looked down, and then at my husband. He looked at his foot in the water then reached down to clean off whatever he had stepped in. That was when the man suddenly realized what was happening and turned to his daughters, who were playing in the deep end, and told them to get out. They were puzzled as to why and argued with him, telling him that they were not done swimming. He then used a more urgent tone, encouraging the girls to get out immediately, without yelling across the room that there was poop in the pool.

The boys and I prepared to go to my parents' room to clean up. My husband decided that it was time for him to abandon ship, too. He walked over to the hot tub to tell his brother, who was by then almost in tears from laughing, that he was on his way to notify the front desk. However, the man who had stepped in the "oyster" had already taken care of that. The lady from the front desk calmly asked everyone to exit the pool area so that they could clean and shock the pool with chemicals. We learned from my parents that the pool was closed for the next 24 hours.

In my parents' room, I worried about how to salvage my little boy's self-esteem. My heart ached for him. But when I looked over, Nick, now bathed and dressed, sat on the bed with his brother, laughing over a TV show. My husband napped in the room's easy chair and my parents had left to walk on the beach. It seemed that I—Nick's mom—was the only one in the family who hadn't stopped worrying about Nick's embarrassing accident. I could see that each of my family members had already put the incident behind them and that I needed to do the same. I decided to hop up onto the bed between the boys and watch TV with them.

When my husband woke up a short time later, I suggested, "Let's go back to the campground. And we can pick up something to eat on the way." Everyone had a different idea on where to eat, but we all agreed on one thing . . . no seafood!

Nick

The Fountain of Youth

by
Betty J. Roan

Monday promised to be the first of many challenging days ahead. This was the day I would take my newborn son Brian home from the hospital. I was so excited I could hardly breathe. My knowledge of babies was minimal, at best. I hadn't taken parenting classes and I had never even been a baby sitter. I did know caring for a newborn wouldn't be easy, yet I felt confident I could learn. There was only one hurdle to cross before I could begin my motherly duties—we had to get home.

Since my husband had just started a new job, he couldn't leave work to pick us up from the hospital. Much to my dismay, my father-in-law volunteered. Harvey was a farmer, more familiar with driving down rows of corn than busy highways. Consequently, he refused to drive on the interstate. I knew we would be taking the long way home, adding much more time to the normal 30-minute ride. To add to the fun, we would be traveling over bumpy, pothole-laden back roads in a car without air conditioning. Fortunately, my mother-in-law, Florene, thought to bring a fluffy pillow for me to sit on. I was already hot, tired and uncomfortable, and I hadn't even gotten into the car yet. I dreaded the ride, but couldn't wait to get home.

While waiting on Harvey to find his way out of the parking lot, Dori and Terri admired their new nephew. Dori once said, "Newborn babies are ugly. They all look like little birds." Brian easily dispelled that fallacy. He was number one on the cute chart. We watched his every move, laughing when a quick little smile flicked across his sleeping face.

"It's only gas," Harvey said, bringing more laughter.

"Look at the way he holds his little hands," Florene observed.

The car lurched forward. In addition to the usual discomfort after giving birth, I feared developing whiplash. I bit back a curse when the car came to an abrupt stop at a yield sign. It would be a long, painful ride home. Harvey waited for traffic to clear and pulled onto the street. I suspected I might be in trouble if the city streets were rough enough to cause major pain. As it turned out, those streets were smooth as glass compared to the country road Harvey turned down.

The car swerved from side to side as my father-in-law tried, in vain, to avoid Grand Canyon-sized potholes. The road was narrow. Meeting a car meant driving on the shoulder, which was similar to driving sideways across a plowed field. My head hit the roof a few times. I'm not sure how many. By now, my brain was a little foggy. I popped the top on a can of Sprite and swallowed one of those Darvocet tablets my hero—the doctor—sent home, "Just in case." What was it he said? I believe it was something about unbearable pain. I think Doc may have been a former passenger of Harvey's. I told myself we would be home soon—*Only 20 more miles to go.*

A good hour and a half later, we pulled into my in-laws' driveway. The plan was for my husband to pick us up after work. I thanked God for allowing me to live, and carefully removed myself from the car. Dori asked if I wanted to carry Brian into the house. I tried to stand straight enough to take him into my arms, but I couldn't. I shook my head, turned and hobbled toward the house, carrying that useless pillow.

Once inside, Dori put the baby in the bassinette and tucked a light blanket around him. I ignored the pain long enough to bend down and place a tender kiss on that sweet baby's face. Love swelled up in my heart as I collapsed, slowly and carefully, into a nearby chair. I lay my head back and closed my eyes. The pain lessened some, at least enough for me to fall asleep.

About 10 minutes later, the sound of a baby crying startled me awake. I groaned inwardly and opened my eyes. I was almost out of my chair when Florene said, "You rest. I'll take care of the baby."

Feeling a little territorial and wanting to be the first family member to change and feed the baby, I said firmly, "I'll do it." Florene sat down to watch.

I gingerly made my way into the kitchen, filled a pan with water and turned on the stove. I located a bottle of pre-mixed formula and put it inside the pan to warm.

Back in the living room, it was time for a momentous occasion and a rite of parenthood—my first diaper change. I pulled a cloth diaper from the diaper stacker and approached my baby boy. His face was bright red. I'm pretty sure he was letting his mother know he didn't like waiting. The tiny cry I remembered from the hospital seemed much louder now that he was home. I spoke in a soothing voice, telling him his bottle was warming and asking him to please be patient, for I was about to learn my first mommy lesson.

I unsnapped the legs of that cute, yellow outfit my mother had given me to bring him home in and carefully opened up the diaper. Almost immediately, a stream of water spewed upward. Since I wasn't prepared for this surprise turn of events, my reaction time was way too slow. I stood stock still, staring, not knowing what to do. Everyone else started laughing.

Fortunately for me, Florene was experienced. She had raised four boys. The moment my confused eyes met hers, she was on her feet. She grabbed another diaper from the stacker and promptly placed it over Brian's fountain of youth.

"Always keep one ready," she admonished, with a smile.

Once the laughter died down, so did my confidence. I decided to consult the expert standing next to me. I asked my mother-in-law, "So what other surprises should I know about?"

"You'll learn," she promised. And with her help, I did.

As the sun settled into the west, my husband came to take his family home. It was time for one more ride in the car. Fortunately, for me and my new bundle of joy, this time Harvey wouldn't be driving.

Betty and baby

Will Pee for M&M's

by
Charles Dowdy

We were on a long, family road trip when one of my kids told me he had to use the bathroom. I smiled and kept driving. We'd just passed both a rest stop and the little sign that said the next rest stop would be 47 miles down the road.

I knew what was up. When a rest stop isn't available and a call of nature beckons, you're forced to run the convenience store gauntlet for a bathroom break. For me, the convenience store is a financial deathtrap. After using the facilities, my little kleptomaniacs usually grab anything that isn't nailed down. Then I've got the choice of paying for those items or testing the response time of the local police department.

I know that despite their constant begging when we're on road trips, most of the time my kids don't really have to go to the bathroom. They might whine like their bladders are about to explode, but they're really just bored or hungry. They know I won't stop for anything short of a national emergency, so they wait until a rest area is out of reach and then lie about having to go to the bathroom so they can rape and pillage the candy aisle in some 7-Eleven.

With four kids pulling this stunt, it can greatly add to the time and expense of a road trip. And time on the road, not unlike time spent in prison, has a way of wearing on you. You know the kind of trip I'm talking about. By the end of one of these drives, my prostate looks like Rocky Balboa's nose. Every vertebra feels like it is made of glass. Every noise from the backseat, every bump in the highway, every stupid driver around me—they all make me grit my teeth that much harder. I swear that I will find some way to get back home, and when I do, I'll never go anywhere with these people ever again! I long for home as badly as Dorothy in *Wizard of Oz*, only I've got sensible traveling shoes and a bad hankering for bourbon.

Urinating appeared to be contagious. One kid said something about going to the bathroom. Then all four complained that they had to go, as well.

The wife patted my arm. "Charles, you have to stop."

I pointed at the wide-open road. "But we're making good time."

"This is a vacation, dear, not a race. Your children need to use the bathroom."

"They went to the bathroom in Colorado."

"And where are we now?"

"Arkansas."

My wife took a deep breath then folded down the page of her celebrity magazine. "Please find some decent bathrooms and stop the car."

The kids thanked their mom and whispered to each other about stealing some Peanut M&M's. That's when I hit them with the shocker. There would be no convenience store ambush. We were doing a roadside pit stop.

A chorus of groans erupted from the backseat as I pulled to the shoulder of the interstate. The kids knew the drill. The rear passenger-side door remained open to provide a little cover. That way, the kids could stand in front of the open door, their backs to the passenger side window, and do their business.

"This is so low class," my wife mumbled.

My daughter always waits out the surprise roadside stops. Usually, my oldest son will, too. This time only the two youngest boys, the twins, climbed out, bitching the whole time. But they wouldn't actually start peeing until their mother also got out and placed her body in front of the car, and for good reason.

You see, I'm not a fan of emergency roadside pit stops, so to show my disdain and to prove my point that actual rest stops—when offered—were the better option, I wouldn't put the car into park, but let it idle, instead. This action caused the car to move forward, slowly. The kids weren't too crazy about it, as you can well imagine. So my wife started standing in front of the car. But this time, she was mad. She stood there with a superior stare on her face, her arms crossed as she glared at me through the windshield. Her attitude made me mad, too, and got me thinking, *Like this bitch ain't got reverse?*

Instead of taking her on, I rolled down the passenger-side window, eager to find out if I was right about their fakery or if the kids really had to go.

"Where's that full stream of urine, little buddies?"

"I'm going," one of the twins said. "Look!"

"That little mosquito-sprinkle of pee?"

"What do you want?!" my wife yelled from in front of the car. "You're making them go to the bathroom with people watching."

"They're straining to make water because they know they're busted. This one's squeezing his little butt cheeks together so tight he couldn't fart a dime."

"You're going to make them have nervous bladders!" my wife yelled.

"Nervous bladders? The only reason they said anything about peeing was because they wanted Peanut M&M's."

We glared at each other through the windshield. Then my wife turned away, tapping her foot as she watched the passing traffic.

I'll be the first to admit that the family road trip can make a man painfully bored. And nothing is more boring than waiting to resume a road trip. Jeez, how long did it take to pretend like they had to pee? Were they going to stand there until M&M's started falling from the sky?

That gave me an idea.

I turned on the windshield washer, not because the windshield was dirty, but because I had decided to spray the washer fluid on the little peeing kids to see if they could figure out where it was coming from. The first squirt arced through the air and landed on their heads. Both looked up. There was some conversation about it. Then they went back to concentrating on producing urine.

I checked the wife. She was still studying the passing traffic. I gave the twins a second squirt, longer this time.

"What the heck?" one of them said.

This one turned his hips a little, gazing up at the clear blue sky while he wondered where the rain was coming from. In the process, he peed on his brother's leg.

Uh-oh.

The second brother looked down, saw his pee-soaked sock, and then retaliated. Before I could say anything, each little penis had become a light saber and a full-blown pee battle was on.

Maybe I was wrong. Maybe they really did have to go to the bathroom after all.

My wife heard the commotion and turned. She saw her two youngest children hosing each other down and tried to rip out her hair as she screamed, "What is wrong with this family?! We can't even pee on the side of the road like normal people!"

Back in the car, the boys whispered between themselves, plotting their way into another bag of Peanut M&M's.

The whole crew: Wilkins, Jacks, Charles, Wayne and Beth

Growing Pains

Onward and upward!

Get Your Ass Off My Patio!

by
Elizabeth Deroshia

Justice has been writing his letters since the beginning of pre-school and has just recently begun forming words. "Wow, mom, dad, on, no, yes, and go" are among his somewhat limited repertoire. I am so proud to see him embracing language and recognizing words I could just burst. And I nearly did burst one Saturday morning when I opened my kitchen door and found the word "Ass" written in rough kid-letters all over my patio.

Justice had really been going to town with the sidewalk chalk. There were stick people with bubbles coming out of their mouths, uttering only, "Ass." There were entire towns labeled "Ass," and even a dog with an arrow pointing to his butt, appropriately indicating where his "Ass" was.

I gasped. My instinct was to launch into a "That's a dirty word!" tirade. But Justice was so proud of his work, I just couldn't bring myself to kill his buzz, especially when he said, "Look Mommy! I wrote 'Ass'!"

I didn't know where he had seen the word spelled out, but I was quite sure he had heard it plenty at home and on the TV shows I failed to monitor like the improper mother I am. I didn't want to scold him, lest I discourage his interest in the written word. I mean, he could be the next Shakespeare, for all I knew. On the other hand, I couldn't let him think it was OK to go around writing "Ass" on everything.

"That's great, buddy! You spelled it just right! But you know, that isn't a nice word," I started to lecture.

"I know Mommy, but I can spell the whole thing: A-S-S. See?"

"Yes, I see, and that is GREAT spelling and you did a SUPER job writing the letters, but I don't think 'ass' is a nice word. Can Mommy show you how to write something else?" As I turned the asses on my patio into "grass," "pass," "sass," "mass," and in a burst of creativity, "assemble," the disappointment on Justice's face told me I had missed the point.

I am never one to thwart creative expression, but there has to be a line, doesn't there? I can't have graffiti on my patio no matter how harmless the intent. This is one of the more difficult hurdles I've encountered in the parenting business. I am supposed to be the authority (ha ha), I'm supposed to be in charge, and yet, I don't have an answer for everything, much less a *correct* answer for everything. I know how my parents would have handled it if I went around writing "ass" willy-nilly all over—with a swift smack in the, well, ass.

Personally, I take a more passive approach to discipline, especially when it comes to language usage. I was an English major, as was my hubby, so we both recognize the incredible power of words, and yet we both believe that words only have the meaning and importance that we *assi*gn to them. We let Justice watch the television shows *The Simpsons, Family Guy* and *American Dad*, with a quick discussion that he can only watch if he promises not to repeat the "bad" words, especially at school. He has agreed to those terms, and so far the only naughty words he has let fly have been flown in the safety and comfort of our home.

I realize this laissez faire attitude isn't right for everyone, but it works at our house . . . I thought it did anyway, until the ass came. *Well, at least he can't write "Kiss My" yet*, I thought as I rinsed the last ass off with the garden hose. But seriously, how long would it be until he was scribbling all kinds of filth around the neighborhood? What if he went to our friends' house and defaced *their* patio? Heaven forbid!

Maybe I should make a more conscientious effort to watch my language. I can't even get away with saying "Oh fudge" anymore because it prompts Justice to say, "Did you mean the F word, Mommy?" He is able to exercise some discretion at this age though, and he wasn't able to do that until recently. It is pretty sobering to hear your foul-ups come out of the mouth of a three-year-old, that's for sure.

I remember one particular incident when we were having an Easter brunch at the preschool and Justice and I were sitting with other students, some parents and several very serious-looking grandparents. We were all engaged in polite conversation when the grandmother heard Justice babbling about the new puppies we had just gotten. They were two little hounds that wreaked havoc in my life on an hourly basis, messing up the clean floor, digging under the fence and chewing on my furniture. "What are their names?" the sweet old lady inquired.

"Their names are SpongeBob and Patrick, but my mom calls them 'The Little Bastards,'" he informed her matter-of-factly. I thought about trying to play this off as some kind of speech impediment, but it was too late. I was busted. I downed my punch with record speed and inwardly cursed the teacher for not having the mercy to toss some vodka in the stuff. I felt like a real ass. And I swore I would watch my mouth from that day forth.

No, I don't have all the answers. I don't know why the sky is blue or how many stars there are in the universe or where your lap goes when you stand up. I'm just flying by the seat of my pants most of the time. But I do know I don't want *my* kid to be the one with the perpetual chocolate-milk mustache and language that resembles actor-comedian Richard Pryor more than children's show host Mr. Rogers. So I've decided that the next time any graffiti shows up, we will just have a very stern talk about what we can and cannot write—pending penalty of . . . oh, I don't know what, but something serious. Seriously. You can bet your ass on it.

Feeding the *Hangry*

by
Connie Lissner

"I'm so hungry and there is NOTHING TO EAT!"
And so begins the after-school fun.

My 15-year-old will stand in front of an open refrigerator teeming with food: yogurt, wedges of multiple types of cheese, tortillas for quesadillas, frozen ravioli, drawers full of fruit and lunchmeat, three different kinds of bread, frozen pizzas, two kinds of peanut butter, three different jellies, eggs (uncooked and hard-boiled) and every kind of condiment you can imagine—and complain that there is no food in the fridge.

This is usually followed by words that make my blood boil: "Make me SOMETHING!"

Keeping up with the food intake of a 15-year-old boy is a very time consuming—not to mention expensive—proposition. My son needs to eat at least every two hours or he becomes *hangry*. No, it's not a typo. He becomes so hungry that he becomes angry, and hungry + angry = *hangry*. Nobody needs a teenager who is angrier than usual.

My boy is capable of consuming an entire sub sandwich, a large bag of chips, yogurt and fruit, and then he'll finish off all of this with a bowl of cereal. That's between 3:30 and 3:45. By 4:15, he is starving again! So, what does he do? Does he sort through the pantry and whip up a satisfying snack? Does he sift through his memories to find one of the endless recipes that I have painstakingly demonstrated to him should he find himself hungry and alone? No, of course not. He waits for me to make him something or he grabs a completely unsatisfying cereal bar and moans until dinner.

I have been saying for years that he would starve to death if someone wasn't there to feed him. And whose fault is this? Mine. I take all the blame for this one. I have gratefully fed him all of these years because he loves food—especially *my* food. What mother wouldn't want to hear her child gush about how good her food is? "You're the best cooker," he told me when he was five, while inhaling whatever dish I put in front of him. That was cute then. Now, not so much.

The other day, while he was begging me to make him some spinach ravioli with browned butter and shaved Parmesan (Yes, yes, I've spoiled him, I know!), I turned to him and said, "No—make it yourself."

"But I don't know how," he insisted. "And you're right here. You could make it better."

"Pretend I'm dead," I responded. He turned to me in horror. "What?!" he asked.

"Pretend I'm dead," I repeated. "How would you eat?"

I could see the wheels turning in his head. He was thinking

to himself if he should demonstrate his limited cooking skills and make a quesadilla or instead pour himself another bowl of Honey Nut Cheerios.

It's usually around this time—right after I've thrown down the gauntlet and demanded that he learn to take care of himself—that I start to feel myself backpedaling. Would it really be so horrible to continue to cook for him while he lives at home? Couldn't I just baby him a little while longer? He'll be gone in a few years, right?

The reality is he would eventually find food or find a way to make food. He likes food far too much to subsist on sugared cereal and frozen waffles. He even signed up for a Creative Cuisine class as one of his electives next year at school. But why would he ever put any of those skills to use if I'm around to feed him? And should a 15-year-old have to?

I ask you, what's worse—not feeding your child who is asking for food or not teaching your child to fend for himself?

I feel my defenses breaking down. I'm just about to break out the pots and pans when he decides to answer me.

"If you weren't around to feed me . . . I'd order takeout."

Problem solved.

"There's nothing to eat!"

Throwing in the Towel

by
Klazina Dobbe

When our kids were teenagers, they always brought their friends home. My husband, Benno, and I liked that because we knew where they were.

There has never been a dull moment on our family farm; our household is always busy with family visiting from Holland, lots of business traffic due to our onsite bulb farm, and, of course, the kids and their gang of friends underfoot. In the summer, our teenagers would have friends over to go swimming in our pool. Most of the time, their guests—especially teenage boys—would forget to bring towels, so we always kept plenty on hand for them to use.

At the end of a very beautiful summer, the boys started high school football practice for the upcoming season. It was late August and school was to begin in a week's time. Practice was held every day, and many of the boys would come over after practice for a refreshing jump in our pool. Of course, they were used to not having to bring towels along, as we had so graciously provided them in the past.

One day, after most of the football team had cooled off in the pool then headed home, there were more dirty towels than usual. Add to that the normal amount of general laundry, and I was frustrated. As I did one load after another, I became more and more agitated. *Why do I get stuck doing all of this laundry and towels when they have all the fun?* I wondered. I stared disgustedly at the endless piles on the utility room floor—mountains of dirty sports clothes, pool towels and the regular laundry of a family of five. *I can't do this anymore,* I said to myself. *I have to do something about it, but what?*

A few days later, I unknowingly discovered a way to resolve the growing laundry problem. My husband and I sat at the dinner table with our kids, having a discussion which included lecturing them on the proper ways to express oneself. This conversation was about using foul language, and once Benno finished with his part of the lecture, I was going to slip in my frustration with the laundry and how, as a family, we could fix the situation.

The bad language discussion was very serious. The kids had used foul words to each other and their father intended to discipline them, especially considering we had a standing rule that no bad language was ever to be used in our home. He explained to the kids that those who use negative words lacked the necessary correct vocabulary to express themselves. It came as a surprise to me when the conversation between the kids and their father became heated, as they argued point after point. Things were not going well, and I found myself upset and very caught up in the unfolding drama.

Suddenly, in an effort to change the subject, one of the kids cleverly asked me where the towels had gone because he and his friends didn't have enough available that afternoon for everyone to dry off after swimming. I was as surprised as anyone when I angrily replied, "Where do you think the towels went? Do you think the f _ _ king laundry fairy took them?"

Dead silence fell in our usually noisy home. For a second, no one knew what to do. No one dared say anything because they had never, ever heard either of their parents use such foul language. I, myself, sat perfectly still, shocked over my outburst. Benno was at a loss for words. The kids didn't move, but only stared at me, with wide eyes and gaping mouths. Time stood still.

It wasn't until I grinned that everyone burst into laughter. Poor Benno was trying so hard to discipline them then I opened my mouth and ruined his efforts to teach them an important lesson. Luckily for me, he also joined in our laughter.

The next day, I bought each of my children their own laundry basket and told them that from that day forward, they were responsible for doing their laundry. And that included the dirty towels their friends used when they came over to go swimming. I smiled to myself when suddenly that mountain of laundry turned into a molehill.

To my embarrassment, my kids have told this story many times. While I regret my poor choice of words, I'm grateful that the laundry fairy came through for me when I needed her most. She whispered into my ear the solution to my laundry problem, so it's her fault that she made me say a word I would never have considered saying without her prompting. She taught me that it is sometimes necessary to express yourself in a powerful way in order to be heard, especially when dealing with teenagers.

Dobbe kids at their tulip farm

Party Shoes and Longboards

by
Stephen Rusiniak

Maybe it's a *girl thing,* but I could be wrong. Whatever it is, my daughter has always had an affinity for clothes and their accessories. It was an early interest in one particular accessory that unleashed what's known around our house as her adventures in personal storage. It all started with a pair of shoes.

For her second birthday, Tracy received a brand new big-girl dress and a matching pair of black patent-leather party shoes. She adored the dress but she became best friends with the shoes. Wherever she went, her shoe-friends went, too, and not necessarily on her feet. Sometimes they happened to be the passengers in her baby-doll stroller, while other times they sat quietly beside her watching the gang from *Sesame Street* on television. One night, they had a sleepover—the first of many. Not long after we'd tucked Tracy in for the night, I peeked in and saw her peacefully asleep and sharing her pillow with her party shoes.

It simply became a matter of routine for her to take her

shoes to bed with her. One night, after Tracy had a bad dream, my wife and I awoke to find her standing next to our bed looking like the cartoon character Cindy Lou Who from *How the Grinch Stole Christmas.* Her blonde hair stuck out in all directions in static electric splendor as her tears flowed down her cheeks and past her quivering lip. And just below her almost-floor-length Winnie the Pooh nightshirt, strapped to the wrong feet, were her two patent-leather best friends.

Eventually though, it was more than just her shoes that began spending nights in her bed. Over the next few years, the area beneath her pillows and eventually her blankets and sheets became a depository for anything and everything that happened to be the interest *du jour*. On any given day, the plethora of cherished possessions found just below the surface of her bedding might include a variety of books and toys, puzzles or rocks—yes, she had a rock collection for a while. A favorite coat or photo might be there with a few of her stuffed animals. And one night, as we tucked her in, we even found her real-life lovebird, Peaches, enjoying some private time with her under a canopy of tented sheets.

Making her bed every morning began to take on the appearance of a scavenger hunt gone wild. As she grew older, though, she learned to make her own bed and eventually the days of finding her hidden treasures passed. As time went by, I eventually stopped wondering if any more of her most cherished possessions were still being sequestered beneath her pillows, blankets and sheets.

Today, she's a teenager and it's no surprise to me that her love of all things having to do with clothes and shopping hasn't diminished. She has, however, developed a few other interests—including surfing. When the time or season prevents her from riding the real waves, she becomes a sidewalk surfer who *hangs ten* around our neighborhood on a longboard—an extended version of the old-time skateboards. It is currently her most-cherished possession.

Last night, we walked into her room and as seems to be the norm, she'd simply thrown her bedspread over the pillows and sheets, implying that her bed was made. Absently, I asked what she'd hidden under her pillow these days. She replied, "Nothing. My longboard is just too big."

Looking at this crumpled and bumpy mess of her bed reminded me of a time when almost anything might be found just beneath its wrinkled surface, and a time when a pair of black patent-leather party shoes slept there.

Tracy with her longboard

The Truth Fairy

by
Lisa Tognola

If you were at a party and someone told you that a winged creature in tights would fly to your house during the night and deliver money, would you believe him? Chances are, no. Because, if you're a realist like me, you don't believe in fantasy, only in real miracles like rainbows, meteorites and OxiClean.

Yet as parents, we feel compelled to perpetuate the tooth fairy myth by fabricating strings of lies about a mythological creature that carries a wand and plies kids with dollar bills in exchange for used teeth. We stretch out those lies until the kids' last teeth come in. That's when youngsters finally get wise to the fact that they've been duped by the tooth fairy. It rates right up there with being conned by the Loch Ness Monster, Santa Claus and Obama's promise for health care reform.

So it was on principle that when my first child's mouth became ripe with loose teeth, I resolved to dismiss the tooth fairy and adopt the "truth fairy," a new heroine who would stand for honesty, integrity and frugality. I would say to them, "The tooth fairy is just a product of our imagination, like jackalopes and Prince Charming. The only thing you'll ever get for a baby tooth is a grown-up tooth, and even that will eventually require filling, bleaching and maybe a painful root canal."

But I didn't want to be a killjoy, spoiling the fun for everyone. I couldn't deny my children their right to senseless fantasy, so I joined the ranks of tooth fairies across the globe.

With each tooth fairy visit, my enthusiasm grew along with my children's. Their gappy Mike Tyson grins and dollar bill dances were priceless.

But there was a price to this fantasy, which I discovered the day this tooth fairy—me—unknowingly fell short.

"What's the matter? I asked my dejected eight-year-old daughter, Heather. "Didn't the tooth fairy come last night?"

"Yeah. She left me a dollar," sighed Heather.

"So?"

"Nicole told me at school yesterday that the tooth fairy left her $5."

"Five dollars! How many teeth did she lose?" To think I had finally gotten into the tooth fairy spirit, only to be trumped by a fellow tooth fairy!

With the next lost tooth, I raised the bar and slipped a $5 bill under Heather's pillow. Still I received no jack-o'-lantern grin the following morning.

"Why the long face?" I asked. "Didn't the tooth fairy come?

"Uh-huh. But she brought Nicole $5 *and* a handwritten note."

"Handwritten note?" I asked, weakly.

With the next lost tooth, I offered up a $5 bill and a handwritten note signed, "Your ever- faithful tooth fairy." Again, the morning after the tooth fairy's anticipated nightly visit, Heather's face registered disappointment.

"I see the tooth fairy brought you a five-dollar bill and a handwritten note," I said.

"Yes. But Nicole got $5, a handwritten note *and* fairy dust."

"Fairy dust!" I exclaimed. How does a tooth fairy top that?

I determined that this fairy had been flying off track and called on my alter ego—the truth fairy. She didn't destroy the myth, but instead explained to my three kids that the value of believing is greater than any dollar amount.

Even so, this fairy sought early retirement. So I called our pediatric dentist.

"Dr. Nelson, when do kids finish losing their teeth?"

"Usually at around age 12. However, there are cases . . . "

"Cases when they're much younger?" I asked hopefully, fantasizing about the day I could finally hang up my wand.

"Cases when the wisdom teeth come in crooked and have to be extracted," he answered.

"And what age is that?"

"Twenty-five," he replied.

This tooth fairy wouldn't get to retire any time soon.

A Tale of a Tail

by
Zona Crabtree

A soft blanket of snow covered a hard sheet of ice which spread across southwest Missouri that morning. Warm in our pickup, we drove out into the pasture to drop a load of hay for our beef cows that were calving.

Our two-year-old Joe Paul stood in the seat between my husband and his dad, Joe, and me. He loved to watch the cows and calves run to meet us, as they were hungry for the hay. Most of the herd circled the pickup, but one small black spot remained by itself on the white snowy expanse. It wasn't moving, and we feared the worst.

Joe stopped the pickup beside the calf and I got out. Our son leaned forward curiously from inside the truck to watch as I checked on the calf. Farm life was hard, and fearing the calf was dead, I was sorry he had to learn the harsh realities of farming at such a young age.

When I checked on the calf, its stiff body was icy cold as

I slid my hands beneath it. Farm people don't give up on their animals easily, so I carried the calf to the pickup and laid it inside on the floor, underneath the truck's heater vent. The calf was alive, but barely.

By the time we got home, the calf began to stir slightly. Farm kitchens often serve as temporary nurseries, so Joe carried the animal in to the kitchen and set it on an old rug in a corner, right beside the dryer. There didn't appear to be enough life in the calf to bother blocking him in with chairs, which was the normal routine. Little Joe Paul watched the calf with fascination as I went about my work, both taking care of the calf and other household chores. At least the ailing calf kept my young son occupied for a time. Our two older children—Gayle, age six and Newt, age five—attended school, which meant that Joe Paul had no playmates during the weekdays.

Later that day, while working elsewhere in the house, I heard a commotion in the kitchen. I rushed in and encountered a pint-sized rodeo made up of a two-year-old and a very lively black calf. The kitchen floor was not meant for hooves, and the calf, suddenly revived and raring to go, slipped and slid as he attempted to cross the kitchen. Joe Paul was delighted with the spectacle, and excited his new pal was up and feeling better.

After feeding the calf a bottle, we moved him to the hay barn. I doubted that the mother cow would take the calf back even if we could locate her, and the weather was too cold to chance trying to pair them anyway. So Blackie became a pet. And Blackie thrived on attention. All three children took on the job of feeding him and played with him as if he were a puppy. And Blackie was Joe Paul's companion when the other two went off to school.

Spring came and Blackie still lived in the hay barn, even though he was weaned and eating grain. Much of that first love had worn off, but the children still frequently played with him. One day, Gayle and Newt went out to feed Blackie. A few minutes later, a horrified scream pierced the air, reaching all the way to the kitchen. Gayle was still screaming as she threw open the back door. Taking a deep breath, she gasped, "Newt pulled the baby calf's tail off!"

"What? Calm down. How could he pull the tail off?" I asked as I held my trembling girl.

"We were playing and Newt caught hold of Blackie's tail and pulled it off!"

"Where's Newt now?"

"He's still in the barn, I guess."

I turned off the stove, grabbed Joe Paul, and went with Gayle to find out what had really happened. *There has to be some misunderstanding*, I told myself as we approached the barn. *A tail just doesn't fall off.*

When we got to the calf pen, I saw Newt on his hands and knees, frantically trying to bury the majority of a black calf tail in the dirt. Due to his sister's hysterical reaction, he was sure he was in a great deal of trouble. It was hard for me not to laugh, but my children were so upset that I tried to keep a straight face. Blackie calmly licked the last of his feed out of the trough and when he turned around, he was, indeed, missing most of his tail.

I put Joe Paul down and turned to my other boy. "Newt," I said as I lifted the distraught boy to his feet, "look at Blackie's tail. There's no blood and he isn't hurting." Joe Paul eased around the calf, eyeing the stub of the tail that was left.

"But his tail is missing, and Newt pulled it off," Gayle objected.

"Remember that he was almost frozen to death when we found him? The tail must have frozen past healing. It would have soon fallen off by itself."

"Why?" the children chimed.

I thought for a moment on how to make them understand. "Do you remember when you put rubber bands on your fingers?"

Gayle was still not appeased. "Yes. You said it would stop our blood from getting to our fingers, and our fingers might fall off. But Blackie didn't have a rubber band on his tail."

"Because his tail was frozen. When that happened, it stopped the blood, a little like the rubber bands would, so the tail slowly died and came off."

My children learned an important life lesson that day,

thankfully without a lecture or losing one of their favorite playmates. Blackie continued to be a family pet until he grew big enough to be turned out to the pasture. And so ends the tale of a tail.

Joe Paul, Gayle and Newt with Blackie

The Little Grouch

by
Mary Beth Magee

Parenting is not for the faint of heart, even under the best of circumstances. When the child in question is a precocious, rambunctious all-boy toddler, the task becomes even more challenging. That was the situation with my son, T.J.

At age three, T.J. was a handful. His natural curiosity and showmanship got him into lots of situations. While I have many fond memories of that time, one event does not give me any warm fuzzies at all. That was the day that Oscar the Grouch went down.

T.J. loved PBS' *Sesame Street* show and all of its colorful characters. He even had a royal-blue hooded jacket that he called his "Cookie Monster coat." So when my mother bought a brand new garbage can, he naturally assumed that Oscar's house had arrived for his playtime pleasure. His doting grandmother immediately yielded the pristine can to T.J., buying

NYMB . . . On Being a Parent

another can to dispose of her garbage, so that T.J. could play the Oscar game as long as he wanted. Can you say, "Just a little spoiled?"

My boy had a great time with the can. Anytime we visited Mama, T.J. played inside it. He loved to pull the lid over his head while he hid inside the can so that he could jump up at people as they walked by. He would growl and grumble in his best grouchy voice to imitate his Muppet role model. Over the next few months, we had many laughs watching his antics.

Then T.J. hit a growth spurt and added nearly 2 inches almost overnight. The next time we stopped at my mother's house, he had to crouch down a little more to pull the lid in place. One of the times he crouched, the balance of the can shifted and it fell over before either of us could grab it.

I couldn't tell you who yelled louder—T.J., my mother or I. Mama and I reached him in a dead heat. When I pulled him out of the can, I saw blood on his face and nearly fainted. He had clipped his forehead on the corner of the nearby gas meter as he fell.

"I'll get my keys!" yelled Mama, running into the house.

I sat on the ground with T.J., holding him, comforting him, trying to get him to stop crying. Blood trickled down his face, but he quieted very quickly. Then, to my horror, his eyelids fluttered and his eyes rolled slightly back in his head. *Concussion! Fractured skull! Brain damage!* All those terrible possibilities ran through my mind as I struggled to stand up with my son in my arms.

"Hurry up, Mama!" I screamed, starting toward her car. I kept begging T.J. to open his eyes and stay with me, talk to me, anything to let me know he was alive and conscious. His eyelids still fluttered and his eyes showed a lot more white than I thought was good. The only sound he made was an occasional whimper.

Mama came running out with her car keys and a clean kitchen towel that I held to my little boy's wound. But lurking in the back of my mind was the idea that something might be broken, so I didn't press too hard, worried that if I did, I could cause more damage. I kept the towel in place with a light touch and kept talking to T.J., hoping for a response.

The local hospital was less than a mile away and we made it in record time. I didn't know my mother knew how to drive that fast! I'm sure she broke several traffic laws en route, but I didn't care. I leapt out of the car as soon as it stopped moving and ran through the emergency room doors with T.J. limp in my arms.

A nurse came running toward me, reaching for him. Other personnel materialized around her, all heading our way at a brisk pace.

"What happened?" the nurse asked.

"He fell and hit his head on the gas meter and I'm afraid he's badly hurt. I'm not sure he's conscious," I panted.

"Let me take him," she said. "We'll see about him right away." I handed T.J. to her, although I didn't want to let go of him for a moment.

And that's when he nailed me. My poor limp little boy— semi-conscious and supposedly badly hurt—opened his beautiful brown eyes and gave the nurse a megawatt smile. He batted those eyes at her, and with a giggle, he reached for the stethoscope around her neck.

The look she gave me plainly labeled me as an overreacting

mother. But I give her credit. She took him back into the work area, put him on a bed and checked him out while I stopped at the front desk to fill out piles of paperwork. I could hear him laughing and babbling to the nurse about how "Oscar fall down." When she brought him out with a butterfly bandage on his wound and no other ill effects to report, I was too relieved to be mad at him. I'm not sure what she might have thought about a little boy playing Oscar in a garbage can, but she didn't reveal anything unprofessional.

Mama immediately rescinded T.J.'s garbage can privileges when we returned to her house. The spare can was banished into garbage servitude for the rest of its natural life. Oscar moved on and other characters moved into my son's brain.

T.J. survived that escapade and many others over the years. The flirtatious little boy went on to capture many female hearts before he grew up and became a wonderful man. But I can never see a new garbage can without remembering the day that "Oscar fall down" and nearly canned me.

T.J.—then and now

The Ups and Downs of Shopping

by
Debra Ayers Brown

It was nearly Christmas and Meredith, my four-year-old, and I dashed into Kmart to pick up a few items. She climbed up into the buggy as I pulled out my shopping list. Meredith, with a golly-gee wonder, didn't miss much. But she seemed content in the cart until we rounded the corner of the aisle.

She turned her gaze to a middle-aged woman with her hair piled up into a 2-foot teased beehive. The woman wore spandex and stilettos. My daughter never took her eyes from the buxom bleached-blonde.

I prayed Meredith wouldn't comment.

As the woman approached, the smell of vanilla musk surrounded us. Her dangling earrings rocked from side to side. She smacked gum to the beat of the *tap, tap, tap* of spiked heels against the tile floor.

"Momma, how about that hair?!" she yelled, forgetting her inside voice.

"Yes," I stammered. "Isn't it pretty?"

I smiled at the woman, whipped the buggy into high gear and headed for the checkout line.

Meredith peppered me with questions.

"How about that hair?!" she repeated. "How did she get it so tall? Can I touch it?"

"No. Now really, shhhh . . . "

After the Kmart incident, we visited Santa at the mall, got Meredith's Christmas photo taken and shopped a little more. Meredith especially enjoyed riding the escalator to the upper floor.

She sat on Santa's lap without a fuss this year. It seemed my baby was getting more comfortable talking to—and about—strangers. Instead of crying, she had poured out her wishes for a new Barbie and a Barbie convertible. She'd even kissed Santa on the cheek. No puffy-eyed picture this year for our holiday cards!

After buying a few more things, we were both ready to go home. Approaching the down escalator, I juggled shopping bags and my purse, preparing for the descent. For a brief instant, I looked at the moving stairway, hesitant to step on with Meredith and all of our purchases. But the elevator on the other side of the store seemed miles away; we were both tired and grumpy, and I personally didn't have the fortitude to make the trek back through the store to the elevator. So I put all of my shopping bags and purse on one arm and took Meredith's hand, reminding her of what we were about to do and how to do it.

Just as I stepped forward onto the escalator, Meredith jerked her hand free from mine. To my horror, I moved down the escalator as my daughter stood at the top, alone.

"Stay there!" I screamed, trying to climb *up* the *down* escalator. At each attempt, the step disappeared and moved me down again. My heart pounded. Sweat trickled down my face as I grabbed the slick handrails, attempting to pull myself up to my daughter. Maybe if I'd stuck with my Jane Fonda workout, I'd have had the strength to vault to the top. Instead, my arms jiggled like Meredith's favorite strawberry Jell-O.

I had to get to her.

Suddenly, my ankle rolled and I sprawled out on the escalator. Shopping bags tumbled down, spilling their contents. My Victoria Secret bras and Meredith's beautiful red velvet dress with the green satin bow that we'd found on sale rode down to the bottom with me and spun out onto the parquet flooring.

Just as I was on my last nerve, a stranger, who happened to be a man, took Meredith's hand and stepped onto the escalator to bring her to me.

Meredith let out a blood-curdling scream.

"Hay-elp!" she cried. "Help! Stranger! Stranger! Stranger!"

Meredith did everything I'd instructed her to do if a strange person grabbed her hand and tried to get her to go with him or her. Watching the scene unfold in front of me, it was both a parent's worst nightmare and a parent's proudest moment. My little girl knew what to do.

At the bottom of the escalator, the man smiled and handed Meredith over to me. He ignored her kidnapper screams, understanding my daughter's attempts to alert anyone about the stranger danger. I smiled back, appreciative of his understanding, and thanked him for his help.

After calming Meredith down, we held hands as we walked from the store to our car. We had experienced enough ups and downs for one day.

Meredith

Lost in Translation

Which one of us is confused?

Cowboys and Indians

by
Susan Rose

It warms my heart when I think about children and how literal their worlds can be.

I remember watching the evening news when I was a child. A plane had been hijacked and the reporter said there were guerillas aboard. *Wow*, I thought, *now that's a plane I want to be on.* I imagined hairy monkeys with spindly arms meandering up and down the aisles while pounding their chests and passing out peanuts to the travelers.

One evening as I drove my young son Max home from Grandma's house, he reminded me of that moment and just how literally children see the world. I had been singing an old Native American song that I learned in music class as a child.

"Max, you know, it's important that you learn this song because you're part Indian, your daddy is part Indian, your grandpa is part Indian and so on."

I glanced in the rearview mirror as I watched the wonder

on my small son's face. I didn't think anything of it as I continued driving. Soon, my son's sweet little voice pierced the silence.

"Mommy, if people are part Indian then how do they know when they are part cowboy?"

I couldn't help but laugh, but it was a good question. How do you know when you're part cowboy?

A few weeks later, as Christmas approached, a lovely poinsettia adorned the antique table in my mom's office. Its crimson petals were beautiful and added just the right festive touch. Mom and I were in the kitchen preparing lunch and Max had been quiet for some time. "He's being so good today," Mom said. I agreed. Much to our disappointment, when we entered the office, the red petals littered the tiled floor. He had torn them from the plant and tossed them to the ground like confetti.

"Max," I scolded, "why did you tear all of the petals off Grandma's pretty plant?"

He hung his head. He knew he was in trouble.

"Clean up the mess," I instructed, and then walked out of the office.

When I returned, I was pleased to see that there were no more petals on the ground. I reached toward the poinsettia to put it in the trash and as I did, I realized that he had taped every single petal back onto the plant!

"Mommy, I fixed it!" he beamed. I couldn't help but giggle at his unique gardening skills and wished that my green thumb were half as good as his.

Soon, we added another child, Chelsea, to our family. When

Chelsea was five, she was visibly frustrated that we didn't understand what she was saying. As we headed to the beach, she tried to tell us what she wanted to do while we were on our vacation.

"Let's go see the big cats," she kept saying.

"Cats? What are you talking about? We're not near the zoo."

"No!" she screamed, "You know, the cats . . . those cat-things that are really loud and they swim."

"Chelsea, I just don't understand," I kept repeating. She was nearly in tears. "Cats don't like the water," I explained. As we neared the beach, she quickly jolted up in her seat.

"Over there, Mommy. The cats are over there," she exclaimed as she pointed toward the pier.

My husband and I looked at each other and smiles stretched across both of our faces. We turned down the road toward the marina where we saw the glistening brown fur of the cats.

"Yes, the big cats!" she shrieked. And although they didn't have fuzzy manes like their namesake, she had been explaining it the only way she knew how.

"Sweetheart," I explained, "those aren't cats—they're sea lions."

Max, oblivious to all the drama about the big cats, sat in the backseat playing with his plastic Indian figures, probably wondering if any of them were part cowboy.

Max and Chelsea

When Mom "Likes" Too Much

by
Liane Kupferberg Carter

OK, I'm going out on a limb.

I'm a middle-aged mom and I love Facebook. And no, I'm not playing games like *Farmville, Kingdoms of Camelot* or *Mafia Wars*. I love it for networking. So when *Saturday Night Live* recently aired a fake ad for the "Damn It! My Mom's on Facebook" filter, I thought it was a hoot. That is, until my 23-year-old son Jonathan cornered me.

"You're all over Facebook," he said. "You've been clicking 'Like' on too many things lately."

"It's not OK to 'Like' things?" I asked. The "Like" button is a thumbs-up feature that lets you say that, well, you like what someone posted.

"It's OK sometimes, but not for so many things. You don't have to 'Like' it every time I breathe."

I was confused. "You can see everything I 'Like'?"

"Yeah, of course I can, it's all over Facebook."

"You mean if I say I 'Like' the picture of Monty Python you posted, it comes through on your news feed?" I asked.

"Yes."

"And that bothers you?" I was still confused. "What difference does it make to you if I click 'Like' on things that I like?"

"When it's my stuff you're clicking, all my friends can see it," Jonathan explained.

"They can see everything I 'Like'?" I know I click "Like" a lot, but how would his friends know? I'm not Facebook friends with them.

"Yeah, if you 'Like' stuff on my wall, they can see it."

"So it's just *your* posts that I'm not supposed to 'Like'?"

"Exactly."

Oh. I thought I was the cool mom because I Tweet. I'm also LinkedIn. Here I'd been cruising the information superhighway feeling like a Formula One driver, and now my kid tells me I'm in the breakdown lane. I did a mental count. I've "Liked" exactly six items he's posted.

"You can 'Like' some stuff, but not everything," he said. "Like, it's OK if you want to 'Like' that I tell people to wear purple to show support as a straight ally of National Coming Out Day."

"So it's a judgment call. Well, I 'Liked' your dancing parrot video."

"It's slippery," he allowed. "Like when I posted that I got a job, that was OK to 'Like.'"

"What about 'Liking' the pictures of your girlfriend Gianna's kittens?"

"Dubious. That's gray area. The boundaries are fluid. Don't cross any boundaries," Jonathan warned.

I didn't realize I had. I thought I was being supportive. I like keeping in touch this way—it's a window into his world, especially because boys don't tend to open up easily to their moms. It's hard to know what those boundaries are today, since we're living in a culture of oversharing. Should we be interacting online? If so, how much? I enjoy using social media tools because it makes me feel hip at a point in life where I'm worrying about feeling old, left behind and irrelevant. *I hope I haven't embarrassed him*, I thought. But Jonathan frequently posted my articles on his Facebook wall. Recently, he surprised me by creating a Writer Fan Page about me on Facebook.

"So when you posted that photo of the guy holding the sign saying 'Sasquatch is Real,' it wasn't OK to 'Like' that?" I asked.

"Well, yeah," he conceded. "That was a good photo. But as I said, you need to stop 'Liking' everything."

"You know, you friended me, not the other way around," I felt compelled to point out. But I was laughing. "Jonnie, I love you," I said.

"Yeah, me too, Mom," he said.

"OK, let me be sure I've got this," I said. "If someone posts, 'Save the Whales,' is it OK to 'Like' that?"

"Mom," he said, surprisingly patient, "I love that you love whales. Just don't love *my* whales."

I nodded. "Got it," I said, even though I didn't entirely. I resolved to leave his whales alone.

"This would make a good essay," suggested my husband,

who was quietly listening in on our conversation.

Jonathan rolled his eyes. "Mom can write her own essays just fine, Dad."

I "Liked" that.

Liane and Jonathan

Nocturnal WHAT?!

by
Laurel (Bernier) McHargue

We were halfway up the mountain. Nick was in fifth grade and generally hiked with his father, but on this day, he decided to hang out with me, his mom, instead of running to the top with his mountain-goat dad. Our youngest son Jake didn't accompany us that day, so perhaps Nick was feeling sorry for me, or even protective. But because of his decision to ensure that I was not left alone in the wild, there was no escaping. Poor kid—he had no idea what he was in for.

"So what are you learning in sex education?" I asked, figuring I might as well use this side-by-side opportunity to ensure that my son was squared away in the birds and bees department. I had read somewhere that the best chance of communicating effectively with the male species is to do so in conjunction with an activity that doesn't require any face-to-face interaction. Examples given included talking while driving or watching television, or during a physical activity like biking, bowling or hiking—such as we were doing that day.

Since parents had to sign waivers allowing their children to participate in the school's sex-education program, I knew that the girls had had their classes and the boys had recently completed theirs. Thus, the reason for my question. As a dutiful parent, I wanted to make sure my son knew that I was interested in what he was learning, be it the ABCs or the birds and bees.

"I don't know," he answered. I could tell he was troubled. Nick has always been a thoughtful and inquisitive son. And from the time he was quite young, he could convince anyone he met that he knew the answer to every question that had ever been asked by anyone . . . ever.

"You're making that up," my husband and I had told him when he was in third grade, after trying to convince us that there was a creature called an antlion. It was something we had certainly never heard of. But Nick quickly proved us wrong, hauling out the unabridged dictionary that weighed as much as he did and opening it to the page that schooled us on the bizarre little insect that preys on ants.

From that point on, any time we challenged Nick's knowledge, he would simply smile and say, "Antlion." For him to admit that he didn't understand something he was being taught in sex-ed made me realize that he must have been positively perplexed by the presentation.

"Has your teacher said anything to the class that's not really clear to you? Because I'm pretty sure I can explain whatever might be confusing," I offered.

I made an effort to sound as nonchalant as I could. We

had a ways to go before reaching the summit, and I didn't want to appear too anxious to engage in a conversation that would provoke him to run off in search of his father. I also wanted to ensure that there was no question in his mind about what could happen someday with a girl if he found himself in a "let's play doctor . . . I'll teach you using my knowledge of Braille anatomy" situation and didn't possess the right information.

"Kind of," he mumbled, sounding embarrassed already. "They were saying that we . . . "

Before he could finish his sentence, however, we both caught sight of my husband, Mike, up ahead. He had already summited and was running back down to check on us.

"Go on," I prompted Nick, not wanting him to lose his courage.

"Well, he was saying something like how we might wet the bed some night, but he called it something I didn't get." Nick was very embarrassed, but clearly needed to understand why something he hadn't done since he was in diapers could happen again.

"How are you guys doing?" Mike asked when he finally reached us, keeping up a slower jog while we continued to trudge up the hill.

"Great! Nick was telling me about his sex-ed class and how they told the boys they might wet their bed some nights," I explained, and then turned my attention back to Nick.

"I think what your teacher's talking about is something called a 'wet dream,'" I told him, glad that Mike was there and could explain the phenomenon better than I could.

"No, that's not what he called it," Nick protested. "He

called it something complicated."

"Nocturnal ejaculation," Mike said as off-handedly as he might have asked, "What's for dinner?"

"That's it!" Nick said, perking up.

And before I could protest, Mike's slow jog turned into an all-out escape from me and my expectant son. "See you guys at the top!" he hollered, smiling at me over his shoulder, accelerating to the summit once more and leaving me to continue the life lesson.

"Chicken!" I yelled. But even though Nick could have left me at that moment, sprinting away from the awkwardness with his dad, he stayed. He wanted answers.

By the time the two of us reached the summit, Nick learned more than any of his classmates would ever learn from the technical jargon presented in class. And since I had a captive and curious audience, I also took advantage of the opportunity to tell him the truth about all those mythical people and animals attached to the countless holidays we celebrated each year.

Discussion on the downside of the mountain was far less serious—Nick's 11-year-old brain had a bunch to process—and Mike joined us for the descent. I felt confident I had provided adequate information to our son in a way that was both informative and minimized any undue embarrassment.

"And don't tell your little brother about the Santa stuff yet, OK?" I requested.

"OK," he said. "Thanks, Mom."

Once back in our truck, Mike asked, "Hey, what do we want for dinner tonight?"

"Chicken!" I said, with a bit more emphasis than was necessary. As if there could have been any other choice!

That fine day, Nick learned far more than he had bargained for, and I learned a few things, too. I learned that for my boys, school lessons didn't always sink in, so I would have to remain vigilant with follow-ups. I learned that not all fathers are comfortable discussing delicate topics with their sons. Most importantly, however, I learned that my oldest son was brave enough not to run away from me when he had the chance. Now that he is an adult, I know that he will, as he always has, choose knowledge over ignorance—a trait that will serve him well in his current pursuit of a medical degree. And no, not in Braille anatomy!

Nick, Laurel, Mike and Jake, along with Guntar, the family dog

The Big Sale

by
James Butler

It is always exciting when our children discover new horizons to explore as they progress through grade school. One discovery—and one that can be both challenging and intimidating—is the concept of fundraising activities such as bake sales, car washes and school fairs. But the real discovery—or better yet, test—comes the first time your child is asked to go out and sell something on his own for the benefit of the school or club he belongs to.

That big day came for our son, Richard, when he entered fifth grade. He came home one afternoon with all the promotional materials for the annual school book sale contest and just dropped the package on the kitchen table without saying a word. I and practically every other child in the country have done the same program at some point in our academic lives.

"Are you supposed to do something with this?" I asked.

"It's for school," Richard said.

"Homework?" I asked.

"No, we don't have to do it if we don't want to."

"Don't have to do what?" I asked.

"Try to win the contest."

I could see this was going to be a long session if I didn't cut to the chase. "Are your friends going to ask people to buy books?"

"They all have a lot of relatives they can ask," Richard said. All of our relatives lived at least 2,000 miles away.

"You don't need to ask relatives. You can ask people who live near us."

"How?" Richard asked.

"Get a friend to go with you and just knock on their doors."

"What if they get mad like you did when the roof guy came?" Richard asked. How does he remember these things?

"Nobody gets mad when it's just kids trying to help the school."

"You can come with me," Richard suggested.

"You need to get the experience on your own. I had to do the same thing when I was your age."

"Did you win anything?"

"Not that I remember."

"Maybe I should find somebody better at it to help me," Richard said, while heading to his room to do his homework.

A few days passed without any more discussion, and the promotional material sat on a bookshelf, untouched. I figured the ordeal was over with before it got started and was frankly a bit relieved. Then Richard came home from school on a Friday afternoon, all excited.

"I'm going out at six," he said.

"You're doing what?" I asked.

"Going out to sell books," he answered.

"By yourself?"

"Yep. Somebody in school sold 50 books this week and none of them were to relatives!"

"Well, OK. But stay in our area and check in after an hour," I instructed. I hoped he hadn't noticed the small amount of fear in my voice.

I helped Richard get all his order forms straightened out and explained to him how to inform prospective customers what he was doing. He practiced coming to our door a couple of times then was off and running. I watched him knock on the door across the street, still in shock that he actually had the courage to do it. I had not shared with my son that I never had the courage to ask anyone but my relatives to buy anything.

No one answered after he had knocked twice, so he headed down the street and I went back inside to anxiously stare at the clock. After 55 minutes painfully crept by, I heard the front door fly open. I didn't move from my seat in the family room. I heard Richard run upstairs to his room, and then heard something crash to the floor. Right after that, Richard ran back downstairs.

"What're you doing?" I asked as I walked out of the family room. I couldn't sit still any longer.

"I'm not done yet!" he said as he flew out the door with something in his arms.

I watched him disappear down the street. I closed the door, wondering why the heck he was in such a hurry. About half an hour later, Richard returned, smiling from ear to ear.

"Look what I've got!" he said, pulling two $1 bills and two quarters from his pocket.

"Somebody gave you a tip?" I asked.

"No. I sold three books!"

"No, no. Customers don't pay until you deliver the books. They aren't supposed to give you any money yet," I said.

"They have the books."

Uh-oh. "What books?" I asked.

"I didn't like any of the prizes, so I sold my own books. Now I can use the money to buy something I like," Richard reported, happy with his entrepreneurial idea.

I was instantly proud and upset at the same time. He was so excited about his first involvement with the free enterprise system that I didn't want to dampen his enthusiasm. But he had to understand he was missing the whole point of fundraising for the school. What was a parent to do?

"You know that the books you sell for the school help the teachers buy supplies, equipment and other things for all the children to use," I said.

"I know. But nobody wanted to buy those books."

"Then why did you think you could sell your books?"

"Because they're *real* books, not just pictures," he said, referring to the books' cover photos in the promotional material from the school's book sale.

Eleven years old? Look out Wall Street.

"OK. What books did you sell anyway?"

"*Mulan* and two dinosaur books."

"*Mulan*? The Disney collector edition of *Mulan* we gave

you for your birthday?"

"Yep!" he said.

"How much did you get for it?"

"$1.50."

"One dollar and fifty cents," I said, pronouncing each word slowly.

So much for Wall Street. We stared at each other thoughtfully for a few seconds before the suspense got to him.

"How much did it cost?" he asked.

"$23.95."

He stared at me for a moment then hung his head.

"Should I go get it back?" he asked.

"Nope. It was your book and you had the right to sell it."

"Are you mad?"

"No, I'm not. In fact, I'm proud of you. I didn't think you were brave enough to do this on your own," I told him, patting his shoulder. "But we do need to have a discussion about determining fair market value before you try selling my golf clubs."

Richard

Remedial Barbie

by
Timothy Martin

Of course I complained. Transitions were always painful for me—switching from meat to tofu because it's "healthier for you," giving up my New York Giants tickets for a spot on the sidelines of an elementary school soccer game, or trading in my beloved sports car for a family sedan. And this was every bit as disturbing—it was the day my daughter stared up at me with those big, pleading eyes and asked, "Daddy, will you play dolls with me?"

Like most fathers, I was lost. Nature hadn't prepared me for something like this. Legos? Sure. Nintendo? No problem. But dolls? Suddenly I was clueless.

Not to worry. My lack of knowledge on the subject of dolls is really nobody's fault. It's simply a lousy little wrong that's been handed down to men from one generation to the next. Men have never been properly schooled in the fine art of playing dolls.

I waited until I was 40 years old to play with my first doll. When I was a kid, I thought they were dumb. Besides, my sister was bigger than me and wouldn't let me play with her dolls. And I still think playing with dolls is dumb. But my four-year-old daughter Emily loves it. She plays with her Barbie dolls every day.

Since I wanted to be a good father, and because Emily and I don't get to spend much time together, I decided to join her. The first thing I noticed when I sat down to play was the absence of boy dolls. There was Dance Moves Barbie, Tropical Splash Barbie, Bubble Angel Barbie, Baywatch Barbie and Hot Skatin' Barbie, but not a single Ken doll in the whole collection. Only Barbie.

There's a good reason for that, I suppose. Little girls spend a lot of time dressing and undressing their dolls, pulling off fuchsia miniskirts and halter tops, putting on stewardess uniforms and gold-sequined gowns. Wardrobes for every occasion. What self-respecting boy doll would want to go through that?

Emily chose Butterfly Princess Barbie to play with. I got Slumber Party Barbie.

"There you go," she said, thrusting the doll into my hand. There you go. As simple as that.

For long minutes I sat there, staring at my doll. "Um . . . ah . . . What would you like to play?" I asked.

Emily sighed, "I already told you, Daddy. We're playing dolls."

Eventually, I began to get the hang of it. We dressed our Barbie dolls in designer clothes, drove them to the mall in a hot red convertible, changed their clothes, and then drove them home . . . where we changed their clothes again. And again. We changed Barbie's clothes more times than I can remember. We changed her clothes until my fingers went numb. Still, there was something special about sitting cross-legged on the floor with my daughter, snacking on Goldfish crackers and juice from boxes, and watching her change Barbie from her spring ensemble to her summer ensemble.

I took on this doll-play thing with a passion born of a higher consciousness. I labored at understanding colors. I worked on coordinating my fashion. I accepted the challenge. I entered Barbie Country, tamed the maelstrom and emerged laughing.

Well, I did OK. Most of the clothes I put on Slumber Party Barbie didn't go together. When I dressed my doll in a purple blouse and orange shorts, Emily looked at me and pulled a what-in-the-world-is-*this* face.

"Daddy," she said, "those things don't match!" Dressing a doll properly is, to my daughter, the cornerstone of civilization. Consider all the things that can be improved just by wearing clothes that match!

Another thing I enjoyed about playing dolls was that you could make your doll do whatever you want it to. My daughter made her Barbie doll work as a fashion model, which included going shopping for clothes. I chose to have my doll stay home and clean house. What can I say? I'm an old-fashion kind of guy.

I also like playing dolls because in "doll land," any and all problems can be cleared up quicker than a bachelor overcooks Minute Rice. Marital problems? C'mon, let's make up! Overdue bills? Heck, just pay 'em off! What? You wrecked the car? Don't worry, honey, the mechanic will fix it! It's enough to make a father want to take up residence in doll land.

Eventually, though, Emily grew tired of watching me send Barbie off to her job at McDonald's and suggested that we do something else.

"Like what?" I asked, secretly hoping she would consider sacking the whole Barbie doll game for the televised Rams/49ers game that was about to start.

"We can comb Barbie's hair!" said my daughter. "It will be fun."

To be truthful, combing Barbie's hair was not much fun. Actually, it was an event on the thrill scale equal only to watching Walter Cronkite get his nose hairs clipped. Besides, I wasn't very good at it. I accidentally kept pulling Barbie's bleach-blond hair out in big clumps.

I was leaving an ever-growing trail of incompetence behind me. After we were finished combing hair, we put our Barbie dolls back into the convertible and took them for a ride. My daughter's idea of a ride was more like a demolition derby. "Careful," I told her. "Don't wreck that car. It might have to go back in the shop for another 30 seconds."

Emily and I played dolls for several hours, and for a complete novice, I learned that there is a fine father/daughter relationship that can be developed while doing things like playing dolls. And I'm looking forward to our next session with a sense of . . . what? Foreboding? Anxiety? The willies? Oh, yes, now I remember: anticipation.

Saved by American Chop Suey

by
Lisa McManus Lange

At 3 A.M., I was wide awake. The clock—and not my biological clock, thank you very much—ticked away. My husband snored beside me, my sons doing the same in the next room. My only partners in this nocturnal hell were the raccoons rummaging through our garbage, hunting for scraps from the dinner.

Ugh—dinner. It's not what I'd had for dinner that kept me awake, but rather worrying about what to prepare for next week's dinners. I wanted to create a dinner so tempting, so original and so healthy that I would win the love of my three men forever. After all, I believe it's true that the way to a man's heart is through his stomach.

I learned long ago that preparing a few meals ahead of time would mean stress-free nights, dinner served on time and calm digestive tracts. To accomplish that, it all has to happen on Sundays: thawing, peeling, chopping, boiling, mashing, browning and freezing. I attempt to have 2.5 food groups represented at each and every meal. But unfortunately, economics, routine and difficult or time-consuming recipes give way to the same old thing for dinner. I'm not talking about boring casseroles, but I find myself using the same recipes as last week, and the week before that, and so on.

But I *do* try new things, masking "the usual" with creative variations. On a typical day, I race through the door after work and still wearing my coat, turn on the oven. I immediately hear, "What's for dinner, Mom?" My response of anything other than pizza is met with three sets of slumping shoulders. But the boys are not rude or ungrateful—the end of dinner is met with words of praise, accolades and gratitude. I wonder how I have managed to raise such well-mannered boys. Then I wonder who is paying them to sing such praises, when only a short time before, their shoulders slumped down to their knees.

It was 3:30 A.M., and I was no further ahead and I wasn't asleep. I worried, wondered and planned what else I could cook. I plotted different concoctions, sure to earn promises of constant visits to the old-age home where I will one day live—and where I will not have to cook.

By day, I scour websites and cookbooks, hunting and foraging for "cook-ahead" recipes— something easy, fast, healthy and different. By night I worry, *What can I make? What can I do?'*

At 4 A.M., I rolled over, begging for sleep, and tried to ignore the pizza take-out phone number that kept flashing in my head. *At least pizza has 3.5 food groups,* I told myself.

To ignore the phone number, I started counting raccoons,

not sheep, and dozed for an hour before my clock's *brrring* rudely announced it was time to get up. I tripped out of bed, got ready for work and before heading out, checked in the fridge for that night's dinner: meatballs, mashed potatoes and veggies. There they were, ready to go, making dinner a snap. Then I wondered why I was worried about dinner, and why I had to check the fridge to make sure our dinner was still there. *Where else would it be? Unless those raccoons broke in . . .*

At 4:30 P.M., after a day at work, I hopped on the bus, switching my brain from employee mode to homemaker mode. T-minus 60 minutes until dinner needed to be served—and that included travel time.

I raced home, served dinner and listened to the praises from everyone before I repaid the kids' kindness by nagging about homework. Then I started to clean up.

A hesitant voice piped up and asked, "Mom, when are you going to make American Chop Suey again?"

I dropped the pot I was drying on my toe. Tears of joy, not pain, threatened to stream down my face.

American Chop Suey, though I have no idea of the origin of either the recipe or the name, was a standby my mom used to make when we were kids. Dad got deathly sick of it—or at least he said he would die if he ever had to eat it again.

Cheap and easy, it's simply a mixture of cooked ground beef, a box of mac 'n cheese (you know the kind!), a can of tomato soup, onion and green pepper, all thrown together in haste and heavily flavored with love. I hadn't made it in ages, and I guess one of my darling sons missed it.

I fought the urge to jump for joy—my toe still hurt from

dropping the pot on it. It was then I realized that while I was trying so hard to please my family, all they wanted were the simple things—the basics. I was so busy and intent on trying to make these fabulous healthy dinners, I didn't stop to think they might just want something . . . not so fancy. So that night I got some sleep and the next day, I stopped at the grocery store and loaded up on the makings for their favorite—American Chop Suey.

The not-so-secret ingredients for American Chop Suey

My Little Piggy

by
Wendy Nelson

The air was crisp with a hint of rain that would now surely fall since I had forgotten to bring my umbrella. Wrapping my cardigan closer, I quickened my pace down the street. Other than the leaves that crunched under my clogs, the neighborhood was quiet. It took me eight minutes to arrive at the school. I was early, like always.

As I waited for the bell to ring, I leaned against the fence that surrounded the play area reserved for the kindergarten students. Within that play area, they had their own separate entrance into the school. It was the school's safe way to "corral" the kids until it was time to go inside or go home.

Even though it was early in the school year, the windows were already adorned with colorful pieces of artwork. Every few seconds I caught glimpses of a child's head bobbing past. When a shock of blond hair zoomed by, I wondered if it was my son. Most likely it was; I could never keep him still at home, so why would he be any different here?

Soon, I wasn't alone anymore. Parents lined the fence, all chatting happily to each other. When the ear-shattering bell rang, I fought hard not to cover my ears like my son did with any loud noises. Within seconds, kids poured out of the school. I imagined that, from the perspective of someone in a plane high above, it might look as though someone had just disturbed a lively ant-hill back on the ground.

The once-quiet neighborhood had become utter chaos. Pam, a mom I regularly chatted with, bumped her hip against mine as she came to stand beside me. She leaned close and whispered, "Do you know what the teachers call the kindergarten play area?"

"No. What?"

"The *pen*." She laughed, and I couldn't help but join her. Most of the parents looked at us like we had something other than juice in the sippy cups we carried.

"It does seem appropriate," I said, trying to stop my giggle-fit. In my mind, I could easily replace the kids running about inside "the pen" with tiny squealing piglets. I spotted my own prize-winning piggy and gave him a wave. He waited his turn at the gate, and only when the teacher saw me, did she allow him to pass.

It wasn't until my precious five-year-old's hand was securely tucked into mine that I let out that tiny breath of worry— you know, the one where you imagine that every kid comes out those school doors except yours. I said goodbye to Pam and her sweet little girl and together my son and I made our way through the hordes of children, flying backpacks and parents pushing designer strollers.

His tiny hand squeezed mine and he stopped. He looked up at me with his blue-green eyes and asked, "Mommy, what's a 'Herbert'?"

Yes! I thought. *An easy question for once! Not, "Why is the moon out during the day?" or "Why does so-and-so have two daddies?"*

"Sweetheart." I smiled. "Herbert is a boy's name."

"Uh-uh." His face scrunched up as if he had just drunk apple juice after brushing his teeth.

"Are you sure 'Herbert' is the right word you're trying to use?"

"Yep, Corey called Steve a Herbert today in class."

"That's strange, why would . . ." Then I realized I'd have to use my master word-jumble skills. My son had trouble pronouncing certain letters, so I quite often had to flip the word around in my head. It suddenly clicked into place.

"Do you mean what's a 'pervert'?" I had to bite my lip to stop the laugh that desperately wanted to escape.

His face broke into a smile. "That's it."

"I think that's a great question to ask your teacher tomorrow."

"OK." He shrugged off his Spiderman backpack and handed it to me. "Can we go to the park?"

"Sure."

I didn't care that it had begun to rain. My little piggy wanted to play, innocent and free, and I let him. And when he was done, we dodged raindrops together all the way home.

Wendy's son, Kaleb

Dueling Over Diapers

by
David Martin

During my years of child rearing, I've noticed a trend in modern fathering—the macho dad. For generations, fathers had limited involvement in their children's lives, particularly while the children were young. Dad worked, brought home the paycheck and was not expected to be an active child-care participant.

However, with the advent of women's liberation and the increasing number of two-income couples, the modern male was required to assume more of the parental responsibilities. And over time, dads expected and even wanted to become more involved in the raising of their children.

Cultural observers have noted the changes this new paradigm has wrought. Men are now getting in touch with their sensitive side and are achieving deeper and earlier emotional bonds with their children. All this, of course, has been to the good. Greater parental involvement by fathers can only help in the healthy emotional and physical development of today's children.

But despite this dramatic cultural shift, some things don't change. Whether it's excess testosterone or some primitive hunting instinct, we men can't seem to get involved in anything unless it's competitive. And if there isn't an element of competition, we'll invent one. That's why the modern dad has been transformed into the macho dad.

When my daughter Sarah was an infant, I remarked to a male friend that it often took me several minutes to change a dirty diaper. He scoffed at my pathetic efforts and claimed that he never took more than a minute to do the dirty deed.

Another male friend belittled my minimal participation in Sarah's bath-time routine. According to him, if I was a real man, I would be bathing my daughter nightly—by myself.

I was even chided for my limited involvement in feeding my infant daughter. Lending the occasional hand to help feed Sarah was clearly not good enough. Ironically, I even began to feel guilty and less manly because I couldn't breast-feed her.

More and more, I found that other dads were judging me. Could I stop Sarah from crying? Could I feed her? Could I burp her? Could I bathe her? If not, maybe I wasn't a real man.

This new duel of the dads didn't end with infancy. Once Sarah became a toddler, I was faced with the playground competition. You don't just take your kid to the park anymore. Now you compete with the other dads in everything from swinging to running to sandcastle building. Sit on the park bench, like I often did, and you're considered a loser.

As my daughter got older, the pressure was on to teach her

new skills. If I was a true modern dad, I was expected to be out there with Sarah teaching her to swim, to ride a bike and to balance a checkbook. Never mind that I was over 50 and had an aging back. If I wanted to earn my fathering merit badge, I had to be a hands-on dad.

Then there's the long-term-care competition. When Sarah was 21 months old, I took her on a 1,500-mile plane ride for a three-day visit with friends. I thought I was *top dad* until I met two other fathers on the same flight who promptly informed me about their younger children and longer trips. My paternal ego was quickly deflated. The fact that there was no extra seat for Sarah on the flight home didn't help. Battling with a cranky toddler on my lap for a three-hour plane ride did little for my super-dad self-esteem.

It's not like I was incompetent. I could carry out all the basic functions from diaper changing to bathing to feeding. And if my wife had to be away for a few days, I somehow managed to do it all by myself. But that was no longer enough.

When I talked about caring for Sarah solo for extended periods, women were impressed. But not men. If I did three days, the other dads had done four days. If I did a week, they had done two weeks. No warm, fuzzy sharing of common feelings and experiences for us guys. This was war.

Sarah's seven years old now and I face the coming years with trepidation. Who knows what a modern dad is expected to do these days? At the very least, I anticipate assuming new duties like assistant soccer coach, dance class driver and math tutor. Beyond that, I shudder to think what will be expected of me. Cycling partner? Computer guru? Marathon trainer? It's enough to reduce a father to tears—if only tears were allowed.

Don't get me wrong. I think it's great that men are becoming super dads. But maybe it's time to also recognize the darker side of the modern father. Let's get this macho parenting out into the open and hold annual Modern Dad Olympics. Then we can really settle who's the best diaper changer, the best feeder, the best burper or the best whatever. And I can finally get back to taking afternoon naps—guilt-free.

Dad and Sarah, then and now

The Little White Pill

by

Mary Laufer

While sweeping the kitchen, I hit something with my broom. It ricocheted off the baseboards like a marble in a pinball game. At first I thought it was one of my daughter Emily's beads, so I continued to sweep, not paying much attention to it.

Eventually, the tiny bit stood still. I bent down and brushed it into the dustpan along with a Cheerio, several toast crumbs and a dried-up grape that had almost turned into a raisin. The mysterious object settled into a corner of the dustpan—it was white, which I thought was unusual because I had assumed it was a jewelry bead from Emily's colorful collection.

I shook off the crumbs and held the white entity up to the light. There was no hole through the middle . . . it wasn't a bead at all! For a long time, I stared at the object between my thumb and forefinger, as if it were from another planet. *Perhaps it's candy,* I thought. But the edges were clearly defined. It looked more like a pill—a little white pill. We had an assortment of medicines in the cupboard on the shelf above the spices. I took down a bottle of aspirin, opened the lid and shook one tablet into the palm of my hand. I compared the two—the aspirin was bigger, yet thinner. I then compared the white pill with every over-the-counter painkiller and vitamin in the cupboard, but nothing was remotely similar.

I stood in a trance, trying to explain the pill's mysterious appearance on my kitchen floor. No one in our family was taking prescription drugs. Could one of my daughter's friends have accidentally dropped her medication near the kitchen sink? I turned the pill over. It didn't look like a prescription drug. There were no numbers on it, no markings and no scoring.

The pill was so small and yet it scared me so much. What if Emily is taking pills like these? It was no secret that she was trying to lose weight. She didn't really need to—she looked the perfect weight to me. But being a typical 16-year-old girl, she'd been experimenting with one diet after another. Did she find some diet drug on the Internet? Just last week a small brown box had come in the mail for her, and I had no idea what was inside.

The pill's surface was bumpy. It looked like a drug manufactured by a shady Internet company. Made under less-than-ideal conditions, its purity and potency would be questionable. She probably doesn't realize how dangerous a drug like this can be!

When I was in ninth grade, two older girls sat in the back seat of the bus I rode every day. They talked and laughed on the way to school then on the entire way home. One of them was overweight and sometimes the kids teased her. I never forgot the morning I climbed up the bus steps and she wasn't there. Her friend was sitting alone and crying.

"Did you hear?" someone asked me. "She took too many diet pills last night and died in her sleep!"

My hand shook now and the little white pill shook with it. I abandoned the broom and dustpan, put the pill in a sandwich bag and drove to the pharmacy at the grocery store. While I stood in line, I clutched the sandwich bag so hard that my knuckles turned as white as the pill.

A woman in a lab coat filled prescriptions for two people ahead of me. When I reached the window, she patiently listened to my story, and then inspected the pill and frowned.

"I don't know what it is," she finally said. "I've never seen anything like it." She wrote down the telephone number for the local poison control center and handed me the slip of paper.

The word "poison" made me feel worse than I already had. I went home, picked up the phone and started to punch in the numbers. But before I finished, I set down the receiver. Whomever I talked to wouldn't know what the pill was without seeing it. If I had to send it to a lab to be tested, it would take time to get the results.

I slowly walked down the hallway to my teen's bedroom. Normally I respected her privacy, but today, I had a maternal search warrant. The pill bottle must still be around somewhere. Maybe it's in her underwear drawer. I just knew that if I found the bottle, I'd learn exactly what the drug was by reading the label.

I opened the door. Jeans and sweaters were draped over the desk chair. Schoolbooks, papers and empty soda cans lay scattered on the floor. The bottle could be anywhere. I wouldn't be able to find it without disrupting the room. She would hate me for going through her things, and if she were innocent, I'd hate myself for doing it.

A school bus rumbled down our street, and my heart sped up. The front door slammed.

"Hi, Mom!"

"How was your day, honey?" I said as I walked down the hallway to greet her. I let her get a glass of milk and a granola bar before confronting her.

"Do you know what this is?" I asked, trying not to sound as though I were accusing her of a crime. I held up the sandwich bag, and she moved the pill closer to her eyes.

"It looks like an Equal," she said, matter-of-factly.

"An Equal?" I repeated.

"You know—the artificial sweetener. It used to come in packets."

"This is an Equal?" I didn't use the sugar substitute myself, but I bought it for my husband, right in the very store where I'd talked to the pharmacist.

"Did you think I was taking drugs?" she asked, laughing.

"I didn't know what to think," I said.

The Equal container lay on the kitchen counter near the coffee maker. I took one of the tablets out of the container and compared it with the one in my sandwich bag. Sure enough, they were the same size, shape and color. When my husband came home from work, he confessed that he'd lost an Equal on the kitchen floor the day before.

I lay awake in bed that night and vowed that from then on,

I would give Emily the benefit of the doubt instead of jumping to conclusions. Never again would I let my imagination take over. But as I drifted off to sleep, something kept nagging at me. What was in the little brown box that came in the mail last week?

Mary and the "pill"

Ready or Not!

Learning as you go . . .

School Daze

by
Ernie Witham

It's perhaps one of the greatest parental lies of all time. You know, the one where you tell your kids how lucky they are to be in school and how you wish you could go back and do it all over again.

Right. Bring back the zits and the raging hormones. Make my legs all gangly again. And please, please let me stand up in front of 35 of my peers and try to give a 10-minute book report based solely on the jacket copy that I just read in homeroom.

But it's what we parents do. After all, we must be supportive. That's why when the notice came home announcing parents' back-to-school orientation night, there was no way not to go, especially since it seemed so important to the boys.

"You going?" they asked.

"Well, I did wake up with this scratchy throat . . . "

"Please," they pleaded.

"Maybe we can stop by for a few minutes."

"Great. Look, if you sign in at our classroom, we get extra credit. Be sure and sign in."

"Sign in. Got it."

"Oh, and here." They handed me a piece of paper with a couple dozen names on it.

"What's this?" I asked.

"Some of the kids' parents can't go." They grabbed their skateboards and ran for the door. "So they're gonna pay us five bucks each to get them signed in."

"But . . ."

"You get 10 percent, Dad." The door slammed. I looked at the names and did a quick tally.

"What's that?" my wife asked.

I stashed the paper. "Business, dear. Just business. Ready to go?"

Desks must be different today. I can remember when I was in school, slipping soundlessly into the little one-piece units several minutes after final bell and immediately assuming the mandatory slouch position. That night I was having a little more difficulty.

I tried putting my legs in first. That didn't work. Then I sat sidesaddle and tried to swing my legs under. No way. So I pushed and I pulled, slamming into the women in front of me then the guy behind me . . . kind of like trying to park a full-size car into a compact-only spot. At the front of the room, the elderly teacher finished writing her name on the board.

"Welcome. Could we come to order, please?"

"I think she means you," my wife whispered.

"Huh? Oh yeah, right. Say, have you seen the sign-in book? I need to get my hands on that for a few minutes, well actually quite a few minutes, maybe 10 or so. Do you have a pen and paper that I could practice signing? Not that I need practice signing my own name of course, it's just that . . . "

I heard a loud "AHEM!" I had a feeling it was directed my way, so I looked up at the teacher. Man, talk about nostalgia. Why she looked just like . . .

"Ernest?" She shook her head. "I should have known. Please don't tell me that you've reproduced."

"Hi, Miss Martin. Still teaching, huh? I mean, not that I'm surprised. You were always so good in math and all."

"I taught science, Ernest."

"Of course you did, Miss Martin. Just testing to see if you remembered. Not that there should be a problem with your memory or anything . . . "

"Are you chewing gum, Ernest?"

"No, Miss Martin. I swallowed hard several times, wondering how much Milk of Magnesia it took to process Wacky Watermelon-flavored Bubblicious through my digestive tract. Miss Martin glared at me until I hunkered down behind my orientation-night agenda. She then turned her attention back to the rest of the group and began talking about the many exciting projects she had in store for all our sons and daughters this year. The guy behind me tapped my shoulder.

"Here ya go." He handed me a note. "Some guy in the back passed it."

I looked over my shoulder and saw the foolish grin of a guy we used to call Slippery, still the current record holder for most football fumbles in one season by a rookie. Today he was a heart surgeon. I opened the note. It was a somewhat unflattering sketch of Miss Martin.

"Is that something you'd like to share with all of us, Ernest?"

"Ahh, no Miss Martin."

"Stand up, Ernest."

"Excuse me?"

"Stand up right now, Ernest."

I wiggled, grunted and strained, and then finally just stood up, taking the entire desk with me.

"Yes. I see the resemblance now. I'll be having a long talk with two young men in the morning. You know what's next, don't you, Ernest?"

I sighed. "Yes, Miss Martin." I waddled to the front of the room, the desk still solidly fastened around my waist, and headed for the corner. Just before I turned toward the wall, I looked back at my wife, but she refused to look at me.

It was just after 9 P.M when we arrived home after a very quiet drive. As we pulled into the driveway, the boys did a few Ollies on their skateboards and came over to my side of the car. Before they could say anything, I reached into my wallet and took out two $10 bills and handed them each one.

"What's this for?" they asked.

"You'll find out tomorrow," I said. Then I limped into the house.

Smarter Than the Average Bear

by
Stacey Hatton

Adventure is my middle name, and parent volunteering at the old grade school is my game. So when the word gets out that you are a giver, just try to stop the phone from ringing.

One afternoon, a kindergarten teacher asked me to join forces with a local program to teach all three classes of kindergarteners about physical boundaries. Sounded interesting. This teacher knew I was a pediatric nurse, had a prior theatrical background and was usually up for F-U-N, so I was a good fit for this volunteer experience.

"You will be dressed up as a bear," she quietly said over the phone.

"Excuse me? Did you say 'bear'?" I choked out with my coffee. For most parents, this might incite panic or deep-seated anxiety, causing an immediate digging for grand lies to bail out of the situation. However, "bear-wear" wasn't a problem for me. Kids often bring out my silliness and we have an understood appreciation and respect for each other. I also reminded the teacher I had spent many years in costumes. Therefore, this would not be a problem—to which she was relieved at having found her perfect sucker.

My youngest daughter, who is extremely creative but terrified of any type of mascot or Chuck E. Cheese-esque machine, was going to be present for the school presentation. Knowing in advance my girl screams as if she is on fire when any costumed parader heads her way—and not wanting her to be known in kindergarten as "The Freaker"—my job as her mother was to protect her. Mama bear had to protect her cub by telling her in advance who the fool would be dancing around with a huge bear head on her shoulders. And it DID comfort her, as planned.

So on the big day, I arrived 15 minutes early to meet with my partner-in-crime (aka, the gal who knew what the heck she was doing), who graciously spewed out my role in 10 minutes and covered my body in not really what I would call a bear costume, but more like a full-on collegiate mascot attire! We're talking a 2 feet by 2 feet head made of hard, heavy material with two screen-covered holes to see through. Unfortunately, the noggin design was lacking in the breathing department. Since this bear was only to nod "yes" and "no," they apparently felt a speaking hole was unnecessary. It wasn't until I was in full regalia that I quickly discovered I couldn't breathe!

If you have been in a situation where you can't breathe for, let's say, approximately 20 minutes, you are either dead or at least minimally hallucinating. I, being the savvy nurse that I am, decided airflow was crucial to my not falling down in front of my daughter and a room full of other youngsters. To not totally freak out the kiddos, I kept jumping up in the gigantic bear head, aiming my pie hole toward the light (aka the eyeholes). With this action, I would suck in bountiful lungs full of O2 to maintain lucidity as long as possible.

Did you know the Kool-Aid mascot has a full-running fan operation inside its costume? Why do I know this? I know people . . . and they talk. But *this* bear wasn't talking or breathing and the main goal was to make it out of the room before this old gal fell flat on her face and scared the peeps out of these delighted children.

As the end neared—and I mean the skit, not me seeing a light at the end of the tunnel—I waved my four-fingered paw with as much mustard as I could muster. (Yes, the hallucinations were a-coming) and headed to the door. I heard the kids yelling what I thought were words of love and laughter and bidding me adieu, but they could have been reciting the national anthem or singing trashy Katy Perry songs for all I knew. I was out of there!

Of course once I caught my breath, I signed up to do this the following year. Wouldn't miss it! I take my volunteering hours seriously—and as a stay-at-home mother, I feel it is my parental duty to help out when I am able, even if I kill a few brain cells doing so.

Some famous bear once said, "Please . . . only YOU can prevent asphyxiation." But let me tell you, next year I'm going to wear one of those camel-pack water bags and have a small oxygen tank strapped to my waist to take hits from during my show.

This parent-volunteering business is challenging, and I've found that it helps to be smarter than the average bear.

Stacey in her bear costume

If Only He Were a Leg Man

by
Elizabeth Deroshia

When I saw the sheet to sign up for parent/teacher conferences, I was very excited. I imagined all the wonderful things
I would hear about my brilliant child, Justice. *He's a genius, a
genius I tell you! You have to get him into a special school, and
fast! You shouldn't be wasting a moment of this kind of potential!*

I envisioned the teacher gushing on and on. *Harvard here
we come,* I thought.

Then I got an odd call. The person on the other end of the
line asked if we could please move our conference time so the
preschool director could sit in on the meeting with us.

*Hmmm. I guess she wanted to tell us how brilliant he is,
too. Good idea, leave no stone unturned,* I daydreamed. I agreed
to the change in times and hubby, Jeff, and I re-arranged our
schedules so we both could be there with the director and the
pre-k teacher, our dear Ms. Rachel.

Not long after the appointment was made, I began to fret.

It had hardly been a year since we were called into the office to discuss Justice's use of the word "penis" at school. Apparently he suggested, on the playground, that another child join him in the drawing of phalluses on the sidewalk. The teacher was not amused. After some discussion, we convinced Justice to save his artistic expression of his private areas for when he was at home, only. I didn't think too much of it, except for a slight irritation. I mean, we wouldn't have been called to the office if he had been suggesting they draw their ears. But I realize my perspective is a bit left of the middle on most issues, and this was no exception.

The day arrived and Jeff and I filed into the office with Ms. Rachel and the assistant director. We looked at the work our son had been doing and the assessment methods the state uses. We heard that Justice was on track academically. And then Ms. Rachel got straight to the "potty talk" issue. Justice had been saying "penis" again. *Gasp.*

"He wants to build things with anatomically correct parts," she said. *Stunning.*

But wait, she's totally skipped the genius stuff—I guess we're coming back to that, I thought to myself while she continued to talk.

"AND," she said, while reaching down into her bag, "he drew these." She pulled out two round, white coffee filters. Holding them up at chest level, she broke the news to us. "They're boobs," she informed, her face reddening slightly.

Jeff leaned over to inspect the white spheres more closely. "What are those, liver spots?" he inquired, pointing to some small, round creatures to the right of a nipple.

"No, they're freckles," I corrected. The symmetry was amazing and the overall form, well, Matisse himself would have been proud.

I looked up and caught the teacher's eyes. Maybe we weren't taking this as seriously as she expected us to. I hypothesized that it could be this lackadaisical attitude that landed us here in the first place. *Sigh*.

"They aren't just 'boobies,'" she told us, repeating the descriptive word Justice had used, "he said they are the fake boobies that mommy wears to work every day."

"WHAT?! I don't wear fake boobies!" I protested. Again, probably not the point. I don't think Ms. Rachel understood how difficult it was for me to take the conversation seriously when she was still holding the two white coffee filters poignantly over her own chest. And Jeff had still not stopped staring at the things. *They aren't real! Jeez, men and boobs.* Obviously he gets it from his father.

"It's not my fault!" I wanted to sob. I had a flashback to the movie *Parenthood* with Steve Martin when the parents were called into the office to discuss their son's troubles at school and each parent immediately started blaming the other:

"You let them watch too much TV!"

"You babied him all the time!"

"You smoked pot in college!"

Suddenly, I began to get paranoid. Had I created a pervert? Would he be sitting in my basement in 30 years stroking his rifle and leafing through *T&A Magazine*?

But wait, I read the research. I knew it was OK for a child to see his opposite-sex parent nude until four or five years of age, and then it was appropriate to see his parents in their underwear. And I knew that seeing the same-sex parent nude actually built self-esteem and a healthy body image.

And the female form has inspired artists for centuries. This is how Italian Renaissance master Giorgione's pre-k teacher reacted when he scribbled the beginnings of his portrait of a nude woman—*Sleeping Venus*—isn't it? What if we had a Cezanne painting hanging in our house and Justice was just trying to imitate it? (*Wait, we don't.*) The female body is, perhaps, the most popular subject in the history of art. This is obviously an evolutionary pull; it cannot be helped. *It's not my fault!*

More likely than any artistic tendencies, I believe that Justice's affinity for breasts probably began as a neonate when he first suckled at my life-giving orbs, filled up his tummy and said, "Ahhh, now that's the good stuff." My breasts sustained him for the first months of his life, giving him food, comfort and warmth. It was a tough time when he hit 18 months and I decided to wean him, lest I have to live as an all-day pacifier for eternity. He gave up the physical attachment to them fairly easily, but the fondness remains.

My low-cut shirts are his favorites, pronouncing me "beautiful" in them as a haze comes over his little blue eyes. He is known to still reach up and give the old girls a "honk" from time to time, and in moments of stress he still tries to sneak a hand down the front of my shirt and cop a feel. I've never really thought too much of these oddities because I understand his relationship with, and attachment to, my bosom. But as we sit, filters still teetering above Ms. Rachel's waist, I realize that Justice and I are probably the only ones who understand this relationship.

At the end of the conference, we conceded we would speak to Justice and explain that those kinds of art projects should be saved for home. Ms. Rachel reminded us that they didn't view this as a behavior problem, but that we should be aware that next year, when he entered public school, it might be seen as just that. *Sigh again.*

I still haven't decided if I'm going to send him to public school or hide him under a rock. We may have to head for Europe where his boob lust won't be squelched. But I guess the best I can hope for is that we can turn him on to legs before kindergarten hits, or at the very least, convince him to switch to asses.

Elizabeth and her son Justice

Bring Me My Broom!

by

Donna Collins Tinsley

My teenage daughters and I battled hormonal changes at the same time, and it was not fun. In fact, I wanted to delete one of the Ten Commandments and add this one: "Hormonal women in the same family shall keep an appropriate distance from each other at all times." I thought I might squeeze the new commandment in right before "Thou Shalt Not Kill."

When their hormones began to rage, my three teenage daughters suddenly knew everything. These girls, who had once looked up to and adored me, began to dismiss me as being out of touch with the real world. To them, I was old. While their hormones increased and mine dwindled, none of us should have been held responsible for her actions. After all, not one of us was the same person she had been before this mutual chemical imbalance.

At times I didn't recognize myself, and I'm pretty sure my friends and family didn't either. I thought I'd lost it. I went from zero to witch in 60 seconds and confused my children by not calling them by their proper names. I sometimes looked in the mirror and said, "Help, my face has fallen and it won't get up." I even wondered where my memory (among other things) had gone and found myself praying for its return. I swam in my sheets during night sweats. Hot flashes came on so unexpectedly, and when one of my teenagers picked that moment to smart off, she suddenly realized she should look out!

My children told me that at times like that, I get a "stress-happy" look. My youngest daughter said my mouth drops open, and then it forms a funny, evil smile. Mind you, this is an unconscious thing because I didn't realize I smiled through gritted teeth. Then, with one eyebrow raised, she says I start ranting to relieve my tension.

I thought I only used this look when they used theirs. You know the one—the haughty, scowl-sneer sort of look that teens do so well. But my girls tell me I also use the stress-happy look when a telemarketer calls the house during dinner trying to sell me something. "No, I do not buy anything over the telephone, especially if you call and interrupt me when I'm trying to eat supper with my family." And I have to admit that I've also used it when I've been overcharged at a store.

Whenever I used the look, I would notice my biologically maturing daughters distancing themselves from me. One day, while shopping in the mall, I saw an ad for "Buy One, Get One Free," good for anything in the store. I searched diligently to make sure I had equally priced things for the free item, but when the cashier rang up the transaction, she gave me free $2 panties instead of $20 jeans. No way was this mama going to let that happen! Wearing the look, I explained that the cashier needed to re-ring all the purchases to give me my good deal. Of course, my hormonal daughters, being sensitive and easily embarrassed, said they would never go back into that store again, at least not with me.

When we went through the drive-thru for fast food, I had to lock the van doors so my hormonal daughters wouldn't jump out—because I, their hormonal mother, have been known to sit at the window and wait for my order when McDonald's tries to get me to pull up front and park.

"Could you pull up and park at the front of the building to wait on your order?"

"No thank you, I'll just wait right here," I said, while my girls quickly scooted down in their seats. It's amazing how fast your order comes out when you do that. One time it only took 31 seconds, precisely the amount of time it would've taken me to pull up and park! It was after one of these events that my daughter named my look "stress-happy."

My oldest daughter mentioned she doesn't mind the look, as long as she isn't the one receiving it. The look can show up anywhere, but I'm afraid fast-food restaurants get the brunt of it. Ninety percent of the time when I check the order, something is wrong, especially if I'm having "one of those days." If I order extra mustard, why do they insist on also adding extra mayonnaise? When I say no ketchup, why do they put *only* ketchup on my hamburger? When my system is in a dither, it can be just too much to handle.

One day, I asked one of my daughters to give me an example of something I did that would put me into the category of being hormonally challenged. She had no problem answering: "I really hate it when you rant and rave at us, but then become a completely different person when you get a phone call from a friend."

Picture in your mind me, with my wonderful Southern drawl and being gentle and smiley. That is my self-image. I absolutely do not rant or rave or yell. "Yelling? You say I yell? My mother yelled, but not me!"

"What about when the telephone solicitors call or the pizza order is wrong?" she countered.

"You know I am very specific when I place my order, going over it many times."

"Yes," my daughter retorted, "but don't you know what workers do to people who give them a hard time? I've heard they spit in their food!"

That little bit of trivia was enough to convert me to eating only home cooking, but I live with fast-food junkies. So when the pizza order comes wrong after paying extra to get what I want, look out! I raise my eyebrow and call the pizza joint immediately.

"Hello, is this Pizza Perfect, where the customer is always happy? I'm not happy! I asked for three orders of mushrooms, not just three mushrooms! Just because I order fast food doesn't mean my kids don't eat vegetables. Haven't you heard about the four basic food groups? My growing teenagers need their mushrooms for a balanced diet. Make me happy or the $30 a week I spend at your place will go elsewhere." By the time I'm done, you could cook that pizza on my red-hot menopausal face!

Surely I am not the only mother who has gone through witchy behavior, but those daughters can be equally witchy, you know? Is my husband the only man in America who decided he should mark a calendar so he could tread softly and buy chocolate for the females in the family who needed it at that time of month?

The comfort of family provided some relief from this challenge of changes. Praying that I could control my emotions sometimes gave me the self-control I needed to put up with the three of us. As a family, we laughed and cried together over our hormonal happenings. My daughters learned to show me love and understanding in spite of my menopausal brainfog and memory lapses, and I learned to show them love in spite of their outbursts.

When my girls bring me a broom, I know they are being helpful and not thinking I misplaced my mode of transportation. This gives new meaning to the phrase, "Fly off the handle." Obviously, it refers to this witch's broom handle!

Donna (second from left) with three of her four daughters

Nobody Likes Me

by
Nancy Hershorin

My oldest daughter, Cindy, was a drama queen. When she was little, I sometimes found her practicing facial expressions in the big wall mirror in my bedroom. I thought she was cute. I never realized it was practice for a life of high drama.

Once, when we visited a girlfriend of mine for a play date, Cindy saw my friend's daughter throw a temper tantrum. She was fascinated, watching the proceedings from beginning to end with jaw-dropping interest. A few days later, she tried it on for size in front of some friends of ours who had come for dinner. She had it down pat, from pounding her heels on the floor to screaming at the top of her lungs. Her father and I were incredibly embarrassed. He picked her up and carried her into her bedroom. He deposited her on her bed and shut the door. He never said a word, but he gave her *his look* and she never did it again.

When Cindy started first grade a few months later, I was

more excited about it than she was. Cindy was my first child in school. I wanted her to have a wonderful experience. I wanted everything to be perfect. I bought her cute little outfits to wear and had her hair professionally cut rather than using my sewing scissors like I usually did. If I had anything to do with it, she was going to be a star in her class.

We only lived a few blocks from the school in a quiet area of town, so I felt it was safe letting her walk home from school. During the first week, I interrogated her about her day the minute she came in the door.

"Do you have a best friend yet?"

"Well, I kind of like Jill."

"That's wonderful. What do you like about her?"

"She's nice, I guess."

"What did you do at school today?"

"The teacher read us a story and stuff."

"Did you play any games?"

"I don't remember, Mom. Can I have a cookie now?"

Looking back, I can see that I pestered her for information, following her all over the house asking stupid questions, hungry for every little detail. Then, to make matters worse, I lectured her.

"Remember not to talk too much, Cindy. Don't interrupt when someone else is talking, either. You do that all the time and other people don't like it. I hope you're minding the teacher. She has lots of other children to teach besides you." *Blah, blah, blah.* Cindy nodded distractedly, squirmed around a little, and then asked if she could go to a friend's house to play.

On Monday of the second week of school, Cindy came in

the door looking sad. "What's the matter, honey?" I asked. She put her head down and wouldn't answer, her lower lip out in a little pout. My heart skipped a beat. I sensed something was wrong. What could it be? I rose to the bait like a hungry fish and begged her to tell me what was bothering her.

"Nobody likes me at school, Mommy. I don't have any friends anymore," she finally whispered to me.

"Oh, sweetie, I'm sure they like you. You just had a bad day." I sat down on the sofa and held her, fighting back tears. She buried her head into my chest. This filled me with anguish. *How could they not love my daughter like I did?* I thought. *Couldn't they see she was perfect?* I told her how wonderful she was and she cuddled up, smiling happily. I put off what I was doing and read her favorite books to her until it was time to make dinner.

Tuesday was a variation of Monday. Cindy told me there was a girl at school who was mean to her and hurt her feelings. To take her mind off her unhappiness, we made chocolate chip cookies, Cindy got to lick the bowl and I made a special trip to the grocery store for hamburger so I could make her favorite dinner of sloppy joes. I was so upset that I called the school and made an appointment with her teacher for the following week. I was beginning to think she was being bullied.

On Wednesday, Cindy came home from school sobbing, telling me tearfully that an older boy had called her names and chased her part way home. As angry and protective as a mother bear, I called the principal of the school and insisted on a meeting with her and Cindy's teacher the next afternoon.

That night I had a hard time sleeping. I couldn't stop

thinking about the other children picking on my daughter. I decided I would put Cindy in a private school or home-school her if I couldn't solve the problem. My husband accused me of overreacting, shaking his head in disgust. "Oh for heaven's sake, it's only been a week. Give the poor girl a little space. She's just getting to know the other kids." But he hadn't seen Cindy when she first came home from school, so I discounted his opinion.

The meeting was scheduled for right after Cindy got out of school. I told her I would give her a ride home, but she'd forgotten and had already left when I arrived at the school. I wasn't worried about her, so I went to the meeting. All the kids in the neighborhood walked home from school in a group and it was only a few blocks. Whenever I wasn't home after school, Cindy would go next door to wait for me.

At the meeting, the principal and Cindy's teacher both said she was a model student. She played well with the other children and seemed to be well liked. They couldn't understand why she was upset and they were skeptical about a boy following her home. Not believing a word they said, I decided that the teacher must have not been paying attention. With a mother's intuition, I could tell that Cindy was hurting.

Driving home from the meeting, my mind bubbling with frustration at what I thought was their indifference, I drove past several children playing in the front yard of a neighbor. They were having a good time, laughing and talking. One little boy chased a girl across the front lawn of the house, waving something creepy-crawly in the air. The little girl laughed and screamed in mock horror, looking over her shoulder at the boy, and . . . oh . . . my . . .

God! It was Cindy! I couldn't believe it. I drove around the block to make sure, half hoping I was wrong, but it was Cindy all right. I parked the car a few houses away on the other side of the street and watched her flirt with the boys and giggle with the girls like she had been doing it for years. She was the center of attention. I had been conned by a six-year-old.

I went home and sat in the living room to wait for her to come home from school. My first reaction was anger and embarrassment. I would have to explain to Cindy's teacher, the principal, my husband and my friends and family that I had been lied to. It would be humiliating. I would be telling the world that I didn't even know my own child.

After I calmed down a bit, I tried to figure out why she did it. I didn't want to think that my behavior had caused the problem, but I had to admit that I'd been obsessing about Cindy and what she did every day at school, trying to mold her into my idea of a perfect child. I felt a little ashamed of myself. I had been an easy target for manipulation. I hadn't suspected a thing.

A few minutes later, Cindy came in the door looking downcast and sad, exactly as she had for the past few days. She was a totally different child than the one I'd seen playing with the other children a block away, just minutes before. I let her begin her little melodrama, amazed at how good an actress she was. If I hadn't seen her having so much fun with those kids, I would never have believed she was lying. She was good, very good. All that practice making different expressions in the mirror had paid off.

Having difficulty staying calm—because I really wanted

to yell at her—I told her I'd seen her walking home and the jig was up. "No, Mom, this was the first day the other kids were nice to me, truly!" she pleaded. But I wasn't fooled a second time. I explained in a way I hoped she would understand that lying could undermine my trust in her and I sent her to her room for the rest of the day.

Thursday, there was no special treatment for Cindy, but I wonder if my little drama queen sat in front of her mirror preparing for her next big performance, whatever it might be. As a parent, you just never know.

Cindy

Figuring It Out

by
Catherine Giordano

"Santa Claus!"

My son John spoke those words in a tone of hushed amazement as we ate breakfast in the dining room in a Guatemalan hotel. It was John's fifth birthday. I was in Guatemala to finalize John's adoption, and he had been just placed in my custody the night before. I looked up from my breakfast and there, across the hotel dining room, I saw Santa in his traditional red flannel suit getting a coffee and a donut to go.

John and I had only just met, and now he was meeting Santa for the first time, too. I think he was more excited about Santa than me.

Here it was, my first big decision as a new mother. Who would bring the gifts—me or Santa? I saw the wonder and excitement in my son's eyes, and I knew Santa would visit our house this year. I decided to play along until John figured it out for himself.

The next year, John was six. I took him to the mall to see

Santa. But everywhere we turned, there was another Santa. I thought I'd give his curiosity a little nudge to help him figure things out for himself, so I said, "We've seen so many Santas . . . I wonder which one is the real Santa."

"They're all the real Santa!" he fired back. And that settled that. Mom learned her lesson. Don't mess with Santa. This was a rite of childhood.

Needless to say, Santa visited our house again that year. However, one day several months later, I thought the Santa thing was all over when John spotted some boxes in the garage with rolls of wrapping paper sticking out of them—Christmas wrapping paper.

"Hey," he said, "that's the same paper that was on my Christmas gifts!"

Uh oh, the jig is up, I thought.

But then, his voice, rising in tone to express his amazement, John said, "Santa has the same wrapping paper we do!"

And Santa survived for another year.

The next year, John was seven and it was Christmas again. Once again, there was the joy of Christmas morning. After all the gifts were unwrapped, he said, "I know that you gave me the robot. I sneaked out of bed last night and saw you wrapping it."

Uh oh, this time the jig really is up, I thought. Me and my last-minute gift wrapping!

"The robot is from you, but Santa brought all the other gifts," he announced with firm conviction.

So Santa survived yet another year.

The next year, John was eight. Christmas was nearing once again. One day he said to me, "Mom, how does Santa get to all the houses in the world in just one night?"

Yes! I thought, mentally pumping my fist. *The moment has finally arrived!*

"I don't know," I replied in a tone of mock innocence. "Maybe it's magic."

His response was immediate. "No! Santa is real!" John knew that magic was not real. Then he answered his own question, puffing his chest a little with pride because he had figured it out on his own. "I know," he said, "there's a different Santa for each country."

A week or so later, John lost one of his baby teeth, and yes, the tooth fairy visited our house. It seems John had been talking at school about how the tooth fairy was going to put a dollar under his pillow that night. As soon as I picked him up from school that day he told me, "Rodney says there's no tooth fairy. Is that true, Mom?"

I answered in my Socratic teacher voice, "I don't know. What do you think?"

His voice was thick with exasperation when he said, "Mommmm, just tell me!"

"There is no tooth fairy, John. It is just a game that the moms and dads play with their children. I'm the one who puts the dollar under your pillow." After a long pause, I added, "Now that you know that, shall I just give you the dollar now?"

He was silent for a moment, and then he said, in a soft voice, "No, put it under my pillow."

Some dreams die hard!

On the last day of school before the winter break, John confronted me again. "Mom, Rodney said there's no Santa!"

"I don't know, John. What do you think?"

"Mommmm, just tell me!"

"There is no Santa, John. It's just a game moms and dads play with their children."

"You mean you put on a Santa suit, climb up on the roof and slide down the chimney with the presents?"

Some dreams die really hard!

Finally, there was no more Santa. I have to admit, I missed him. Before the big reveal, I could count on every December bringing out the best in my little boy. He was so well behaved. I confess, I was not above using Santa to get that good behavior. As a single mother, I'd do just about anything for 25 days of good behavior. And what about John's loooong Christmas list, the one he used to give to Santa? Once he learned that there was no Santa, he started to give the list to me!

My story ends with Easter. "Mom, there's no tooth fairy, and there's no Santa—and that means there's no Easter Bunny either, right?!" This time he was justifiably proud of himself. He had figured it out on his own.

John turned 23 last December. As I write this, Halloween is not that far off, and John has yet to ask about the Great Pumpkin. It's just a matter of time.

Santa and John

Mr. Know-It-All

by
Stacey Gustafson

Nothing is scarier than walking into your son's bedroom to catch him reading the Department of Motor Vehicles booklet. At that moment, I knew I had to find the Excedrin.

I hadn't reminded my son that he was approaching the eligible age to take the DMV test, because imagining him behind the wheel of the family van caused me stomach ulcers and nightmares. His personality was spontaneous, excitable and emotional. And then there were the insurance issues. Teenage boys are considered careless drivers with out-of-control insurance premiums. *Maybe he could wait and get his license after he found a job or got married,* I thought.

"I want to begin my online classes," he announced one morning, spinning gum around his finger.

"It's too soon," I said. "You can't take the test until you're 15 and a half."

"That's in two weeks, he replied."

Busted.

The next time he asked, I tried the Stupid Mom approach.

"I want to start my online driver's education class today," he said, as he tossed a cupcake into the air.

"Lost my Visa," I said. "Try again next weekend."

My procrastination technique sounded as weak as Lance Armstrong without performance-enhancing drugs. Let me explain the reasons for my deception.

My son's ideas of car safety rival the two-day, vacation-turned-nightmare in the movie *Thelma and Louise*. For example, as I drove home from the mall, the streetlight turned green, yet the car in front of us remained stationary.

"Get real close and push him across," he said, irritation wrinkling his forehead.

Oh, crap! Did he just say what I thought he said?

And he did not seem to think the speed limit and rules of the road applied to him.

"Don't let that car beat you to the stop sign," he said in a loud voice.

Yowza!

Finally, I caved in to his request to start his online training. He was a man on a mission, a boy possessed. As he got closer to completing his online classes, his attitude got even worse. Mr. Know-It-All criticized my driving every chance he got, but I noticed that he had learned a thing or two.

"Ten and two," he said, glancing out the window.

"What?" I asked, peeking at him from the corner of my eye.

"Hands. Ten and two," he repeated.

"Thanks," I said, feeling as if I were the one about to take the driving test.

The drive to school and back resulted in constant reprimands. Ol' Eagle Eyes never missed a moment to remind me about The Rules. "Hey, you're blocking the crosswalk," he said, as he stared straight ahead. "One point. You failed the test."

And he caught every driving infraction. "You're going eight miles over the speed limit," he sternly warned.

"No, I'm not," I said, pursing my lips. "This area is 45 miles per hour."

"You're not outside the school zone yet," said Mr. Know-It-All. "Two points off."

And he provided public service announcements free of charge. "Did you change the address on your license yet? You need to do that when you move."

"Nah, too busy."

"It's a $500 fine and three points if you don't change it within 10 days. You're breaking the law."

And he believed he knew all the shortcuts, too. "You're going the wrong way. Turn right, left, left, through the intersection and north on Highway 680."

A regular Rand McNally, I fumed silently. But at the same time, I was proud of my boy—he was really serious about becoming a good and safe driver.

"Are you listening to me?" he asked.

"Yes, dear," I said, smiling to myself.

He studied in the car, after school, at dinner, in the bathroom, at every available moment, intent on finishing his driver's test before he turned the magic age. Final online score:

89 percent. An official certificate arrived in the mail the next week. He circled the kitchen island like a one-eyed cheetah, anxious to start his behind-the-wheel lessons.

"Ready to take the written test at the DMV?" I asked, grabbing the car keys.

"I'm ready," he said, hopping from foot to foot. "Do I have to pay for it?"

"Yep, that will be $50." *Or two points*, I thought to myself.

Mr. Know-It-All and Mom

Ready to drive, at last!

It's How You Play the Game

by
Cynthia Ballard Borris

"Mommy!" Karl said, running from the dugout, his arms full of gear. "Look what the coach gave us."

I took the pint-size blue and gold jersey and held it up in the breeze. The front had "San Lorenzo Little League" written on it and the back had "Buck Henry's B&G."

"Your sponsor is the bar and grill?" I glanced around a sleeve and eyed my nine-year-old shortstop.

He grinned. "Now all your friends can root for our team," he said. I shuddered as I visualized betting pools and score-boards with little squares.

"Guess what else we got." Socks, a sweatshirt and a medium-size supporter tumbled to the ground. He shuffled through the pile, suddenly popping up like a fly ball, holding a package under my nose. "Candy!"

"Fundraiser chocolate bars?" I read the item count: 24 bars per box at $1 each.

"For the team." He peeled open a box, snatched a long bar and ripped back the wrapper. "And the person who sells the most gets a 10-pound candy bar."

I snagged a second liability from his hand. "How many boxes do you have?"

"Five!" His eyes sparkled.

I gulped and did the math in my head: *120, minus one.*

"We can come back for more. Coach has plenty."

"I bet he does." I waved to the enthusiastic coach and be-grudgingly hauled away boxes, begging to define the *fun* in fundraiser.

On the ride home, I tapped my fingers on the steering wheel and mulled to myself as boxes of calories weighed down the backseat. *Maybe take them to work? Nah, established terri-tory reigned during peak season.* Key spots for selling fundraiser products were already overwhelmed by co-workers with se-niority; I was a newbie. *Grandma and Grandpa?* No, the 100-mile ride pushed the profit margin to the negative column. I racked my brain for creative disbursement.

"I have an idea." I turned into our driveway and shared, "You and your sister can stand outside Buck Henry's and sell candy." *After all,* I thought, *Buck is a co-conspirator. He might as well get into the game.*

"Cool, I'll go tell Erin." Karl scooted out of the car, arms overloaded with Little League dreams to share with his little sister. I hustled behind, eager for a quick sale.

Inside, I dug through drawers. I tossed the kids their bright yellow shorts and plastic helmets, each with a Oak-land A's baseball team sticker. Might as well invite the big league into the little league fundraiser. After all, these are their future players.

"Why do we need to wear these?" Erin peeked out from the oversized helmet.

Karl pulled the trunks away from his skinny legs and frowned. "I look like a lemon."

"Marketing," I said. A final search netted a pennant flag featuring an elephant lifting its trunk and tooting, "Go A's."

"I'm not holding that thing," Karl said, backing away, palms planted high in protest.

I sensed a player strike. "Erin?"

"No way!" Her golden curls bounced in negative agreement. She stood alongside her brother. *Two against one.*

I conceded the battle and rallied on. "Got your money box? Candy?" We then headed out to put our plan into motion.

Outside the tavern, Karl held the candy box while Erin cradled the money container. I sat in the car and signaled the kids of potential customers.

A customer! I made eye contact with Karl. We locked stares. I tapped my chest, stroked my fingers down my arm and tipped my nose. He pulled his right ear lobe. Message received. The customer was at the plate. I watched and waited. Nada. *What? No purchase? Probably a low-carb guy.*

A couple stopped; the woman spoke to Karl. He stood soldier-stiff, not even popping his gum. Erin huddled by her older brother, quiet for a first-grade chatterbox. Stalemate. A shared glance and the twosome walked away, not carrying any extra calories.

A patron exited the grill. "What're you selling?"

Karl's mouth dropped open as he shuffled on his feet, but no words of sale escaped. With a shrug, the man sauntered away. *Three up, three down.* I called the kids to the car window. "What's wrong?"

The freckles on Karl's face outshone the fear in his pale blues. "You said never talk to strangers." Trapped by a technicality, I slumped in the seat. *There's got to be a fundraiser clause in the parenting handbook.*

"Get in the car. I have an idea."

"Not another idea," Erin whispered, reconsidering her duty to her brother.

After a quick trip to the store for marking pens and construction paper, we were back at our spot with an added prop—a Little Slugger bat posed over Karl's right shoulder. Good touch. Brother and sister on the same game plan, ready to go for the win.

"Aren't they adorable? What's in the box?" A crowd gathered. *Bases loaded.*

On cue, Erin flashed a large sign: "Candy bars $1 each." A woman opened her purse and Washington crossed home plate.

"Where's the money going?" Buck's cook jingled four quarters in his palm.

Without saying a word, Karl flipped a second piece of bright construction paper. Purple crooked letters answered: "Support Little League Baseball." Karl's face lighted with the sale. He pulled out a third sign: "Thank you."

Coins and dollars dropped into the box; chocolate bars exited right and left. In the night air, not a word was spoken to a stranger. *Score one for Mom.*

At evening's end, I flung the last empty container into the garbage bin, pulled three candy bars from my pocket and said to my winning brother-and-sister team, "It's all in how you play the game that makes you a winner." Then I gave them each a victory candy bar and kept one for myself.

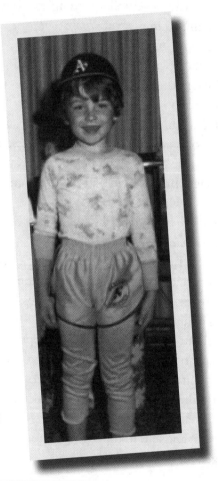

Karl

CHAPTER SIX

You Just Never Know

Paying the price, again and again.

The Condom

by

Mary Laufer

When you have kids, they drop bombs on you in the least likely places. This bomb dropped on me one morning in the bathroom.

I was gathering wet towels, preparing to throw a load into the washer, when I noticed my son's forgotten wallet on the counter by the sink. At first I worried that Andy wouldn't be able to pay for his lunch at school. *Maybe he could borrow money from a friend,* I thought. Then something about the wallet drew my attention—a raised ring indented in the leather from the inside. I knew what was making this circular impression in the wallet, but even with the evidence sitting right in front of me, I still found it hard to believe.

Andy was hardly my little boy anymore. He was 17, almost 6 feet tall and weighed 175 pounds. He was driving, he was dating and I suspected that he was watching R-rated movies. But it never occurred to me that he was having sex.

I'd had my first inkling of him as a sexual being just a few weeks before when a neighbor called me, laughing on the phone. "Mary! I've got to tell you! I saw this cute guy at the four-way stop. What a hunk! Then I realized he was your son!"

I almost fell over. That night, I warned Andy to be on the lookout for 40-year-old divorced women who might have the hots for him. He rolled his eyes, embarrassed. He didn't think I was serious, which was somehow reassuring.

Andy honestly seemed as innocent as he was years ago when his hamsters were doing what came naturally and he came running to me yelling, "The male is hurting the female!" I had to explain to him what was happening and assure him that the female was not being harmed. Later, as he got older, situations on TV gave me the opportunity to bring up related topics—a man's responsibility when he fathers a child and the risk of sexually transmitted diseases. Andy was more uncomfortable discussing these things than I was. He'd cut me short and say, "We learned about that in school, Mom."

I stared at the indentation in the wallet. *Shouldn't I be glad that he's aware of the consequences, that he's not having unprotected sex?* This rolled-up sheath could save him from herpes or AIDS or keep him from being rushed into a teen marriage. But common sense nudged me. *This rolled-up sheath could also slip off or tear, couldn't it? Nothing is 100 percent safe. And emotionally, Andy certainly isn't ready for sexual intercourse.* I had hoped he'd save that for marriage. How would I ever trust him alone in the house again, knowing he might bring a girl to his bed?

I wondered who she was. No doubt one of the sweet voices who called and asked for Andy. He'd race to his room, pick up the extension and shout for me to hang up. When we were gone, they left messages on the answering machine: "This is so-and-so" and "This is you-know-who." He took one of them to the homecoming dance, but she wasn't a steady girl. I couldn't imagine him having casual sex with her in the backseat of our car.

Yet what about the night he didn't get in until 1 A.M.? He'd said that he took home a girl who was crying because she broke up with her boyfriend, and that she lived on the other side of town. Was that just a story? He had me believing that he was a knight in shining armor, when quite possibly he'd just gone out parking.

Perhaps now I was simply recalling what I had done when I was 17 and the stories I had made up to tell my own parents. I wasn't so old that I couldn't remember what it was like to be a teenager. When my mother got involved in my business, I wailed bitterly, "You have no right to intrude into my private life!" I'd heard the same indignation in Andy's voice. So many times he'd been angry with me for coming into his room to empty the wastebasket, even when I explained that ants feast on the crumbs in his granola bar wrappers. He said that he didn't care if ants invaded his room and that I must stay out.

This was not his bedroom though—this was the bathroom, and he'd left his wallet there in plain sight. I picked it up and turned it over in my hands. The leather was worn, the dark, dirty circle ingrained into it. The condom must have been there a long time. Maybe he just carried one around to impress his friends.

He would be furious with me if he knew what I was doing. Part of me was furious with myself. It was strange to see things from two perspectives now, yet the "mother" point of view was slowly shutting the other out. Where does a child's privacy end and a parent's rights begin? How do you distinguish concern from prying? My parents had one answer for both of these questions, and it began with, "As long as you're living under this roof . . . "

I opened the two flat folds of the wallet. My fingers walked past the dollar bills and touched what was in the compartment on the other side of the flap. No foil pouch. No rubber. It felt like an old-fashioned wooden nickel. As I the pulled out the small disk, I recognized it, something my sister had given Andy a few years ago when she had come to visit. It looked like a coin but had a gold cross on one side and these words on the other: "I carry this cross in my pocket to remind me that Jesus Christ is my Savior."

In my mind I heard Andy saying, *You don't have a clue, Mom.* And he was right.

I placed the disk back where I'd found it, making sure that it fit exactly into the indentation again. Then I returned the wallet to the counter by the sink. No bombs had dropped after all. Shaking my head, I gathered the wet towels into my arms.

Mary and the suspect wallet

Huckleberry Hounds

by
Kathe Campbell

Whoops and yells echoed up and down Hannibal Street as our little children pedaled their bikes, hollering that their dad was about to finish the playhouse. My husband, Ken, had finally taken leave of the decking on our new home to concentrate on the little ranch-style dwelling he promised to build our children before summer's end. Having one's own private digs at the far southeast corner of our sprawling backyard was as good as it gets in a neighborhood full of little girls.

"Where will our window be?" piped up our youngest as Dad the builder screwed in the last pieces of bright red metal roofing.

"Right here on the east side to catch the morning sun, and maybe one on the west for the sunsets. How does that sound?" their dad quizzed them while concentrating on measurements.

It all started with our transfer to Montana, a move that excited us, as nature lovers, to our very cores. Our young family fell in love with a life of leisure in the great outdoors, far from big city trappings.

Though we sometimes missed the sophistication of metropolitan culture, we settled into a lifestyle most folks only dream about. Then the ugly "transfer" word sprang up. A transfer back to Seattle was imminent. There was groaning and moaning from the cheap seats as great wails loomed over the dinner table, lamenting missing their sports, Brownie Scouts and, most of all, their friends. We didn't want to leave the Montana lifestyle we loved so much, so as a family, we made the decision to say goodbye to Dad's big-city corporate job and not return to Seattle. We then rolled out the welcome mat for friends and relatives at our Montana Shangri-La.

Three years prior, our fun-loving neighbors and we had brewed homemade wines using local huckleberries. Any vessel that could be corked qualified to hold our fermenting and coveted vintages. Up and down our street, our fermenting wine gurgled in laundry rooms, garages and basements. We celebrated New Year's with popping corks and sparkling secondary fermentation that produced perfect spume. But unhappily, most of us had trouble taming our big jugs of the reds. Despite hours of poring over how-to manuals, there surfaced a glitch.

One shelf in our big new garage was home to the anvil chorus of those sorry reds I had hoped would disappear. Instead of fermenting gracefully and sipping like nectar of the gods, the liquor had become the stuff of lacquer. Rip-roarin' headaches caused near blindness and morning distempers with anyone who dared speak. I had begged Ken to let me toss the stuff out, but he was adamant. "We were lucky to pluck huckleberries ahead of the bears," he insisted.

Now and then he braved the opening of one or two bottles on special occasions, while the younger set grimaced and groaned in unpalatable pain. "What are you guys celebrating with that awful smelling stuff anyhow?" came young challenges. "You're not going to serve it to company, are you?" No one could have felt more secure knowing that our darlings would rather commit hara-kiri than make friends with that god-awful wild huckleberry stuff.

When the playhouse was finally carpeted and furnished, and bright curtains hung, the girls moved in with the dogs to test their courage 85 feet away from the safety of the house and their bedrooms. They turned on the FM radio while a soft rain doused their new metal roof with soft splatters. Best friends fairly waited in line for a sleepover invite, not that much sleep ever took place with a mischievous older brother and his buddies skulking about the playhouse's premises.

An evening came when Ken and I would attend a wedding and our eight-year-old asked to invite a couple friends for a sleepover in the new pad. Without even a second thought, I agreed. "Sure, take your sleeping bags, pillows and flashlights. We'll be home around 10 or so. There are snacks in the pantry and extra soda pop in the garage should you run out."

The giggling and gossiping on the lips of three third graders enchants. The giggling and gossiping on the lips of three third graders with a snoot full jades that charm somehow. Because those awful wine jugs were languishing in close proximity to the soda, the temptation had obviously been too great. We discovered their foray into our forbidden liquid fruit offerings when we returned home. It hardly took a genius to figure it out.

So what to do? Swallow our pride and take the little pie-eyed guests home with awkward apologies, or hide them away in big warm beds while they sobered up back to the land of the living?

"Well, good morning sleepyheads," I said as I stirred late-morning pancake batter for the ravenous survivors of a first-time binge that never passed over anyone's lips again. And I finally got my way parting company with the contents of those wretched jugs, though Ken and I often laughingly recall that night of the schnockered huckleberry hounds.

The bicycle girls, 1968

Karma, Kickbacks and Kids

by

Carole Ann Moleti

Zoe stamped her foot and whined like a fire engine siren. "I want to go boat now!"

"We have to wait our turn, sweetie." Her mother tousled the toddler's blond curls and chatted with a friend while the tantrum escalated. Zoe finally collapsed into a backward death spiral, screaming, thrashing, kicking.

My beau and I stood in line in the verdant Boston Public Garden, patiently waiting to board the swan boats. We rolled our love-struck eyes, annoyed that a romantic spring afternoon had been disrupted so.

"If you don't stop, Zoe, we'll have to leave." Her mother's voice was far too soft and lilting to control the brat.

Zoe didn't stop. In fact, being ignored made her cry even harder. Her mother finally carried her off, with Zoe still howling and contorting like one possessed.

"We'll never have kids like that," I said to John who, two

years later, became my husband.

I returned home pregnant from a delicious three-week honeymoon in Italy. The puking started immediately, doing serious damage to newlywed passion.

We were thrilled to welcome our first son Nicholas to the world. I fell into the parent trap and lost my head to the guillotine—homemade organic baby food, elaborate birthday parties for 50, Lego sets that, when assembled, covered the dining room table. And a vocabulary that seriously overused the platitude "good job" for every physical milestone, scribble on a paper and hit on the potty. "Use your words" became my mantra when Nicholas strayed from the path and did things like whacking a friend who wanted to play with his train set.

It wasn't until our second son, Adam, was born that the fallout from those youthful words uttered in the Boston Public Garden sprayed me in the face like an undiapered baby boy.

We arrived home from the hospital and I plopped on the sofa to nurse the newborn.

"So when is he going back?" Nicholas, now a loquacious two-year-old, asked.

"Oh, Nicky. Adam is ours forever. He isn't going back to the hospital." I struggled not to cry, denying that the sense of impending doom could be due to anything more than being pumped up on hormones and the baby barracuda drawing blood with each chomp of his toothless gums.

Nicholas cocked his head to one side and wagged a finger. "Oh, no. He has that crib on wheels there. With his name on it. They'll be looking for him. He has to go back right now."

John and I exchanged glances. A flicker of worry crossed

my husband's face.

"Perfectly normal," I insisted, recalling lectures about the psychology of firstborns who had been replaced.

More negative kickbacks accumulated while I laughed about it and told the story to all my friends and relatives. In the weeks that followed, Nicholas pushed his brother "higher, higher" in the swing, stuffed Cheerios into Adam's mouth, threw pillows and toys into the crib and, when he bent over to kiss the baby, pinched him.

It took skill and courage to take the two of them out together. One fine summer day, while pushing the double stroller with Adam sleeping in the back, Nicholas stood up in the front, faced backward and dropped metal toy trains on top of his brother.

A young man, as innocent or stupid as I had been that fateful day in Boston, laughed and shook his head as he surveyed the scene. "You certainly have your hands full."

Eat my cookie crumbs, I thought. *Just wait until you have children of your own.*

Every picture of the two boys shows a wide-eyed infant shocked by the snickering brother victimizing him from behind. As Adam learned to walk, video surveillance shows Nicholas tripping him. No structure Adam ever built was left untoppled.

As they grew, the occasional peaceful moment while they played or watched a movie together would evaporate in an instant, with one hitting the other with a yardstick, the other retaliating and chasing his brother with a baseball bat.

They matured into more daring adventures like hailing

down cars on the street to scalp Mets tickets, which netted them a counterfeit $100 bill—all under the watchful eye of the baby sitter.

I had to get in between both boys once and, while pushing them apart, the now taller-than-their-mother teenagers almost took me out while punching at each other. We're from New York City, so quick reflexes and some Bronx charm aborted the attack. "Go ahead, hit me and you won't live to brag about it," I said.

I am an upstanding citizen, so a lot of good karma swirls around me. The bad stuff finally dissipated, along with a number of nerve endings and brain cells. Keeping the boys separated as much as possible avoided many opportunities to incur the wrath of the gods. Their sister, too little, too female and too cute to incite competition, diffused the ticking bomb. Maya, when asked not to do something, always says, "OK, Mommy." And she really means it.

Maya, John and I just had a vacation. The boys didn't go with us—Adam was getting the crap beat out of him in football camp and Nicholas was pounding out death metal at a music school intensive. At breakfast one morning, a tow-headed boy at the neighboring table, about age two, spilled juice all over the floor but still insisted on holding the cup himself. He crumbled a muffin all over the floor, and then started to cry. When his mother took the remnants away, the protests escalated into shrieks. My daughter looked at me and put her hands over her ears.

"Little kids act like that sometimes, Maya," I said. I told her about the time Nicholas, on a dare from his brother, chugged six glasses of soda. He then chucked up all over the dining room on his way to the restaurant buffet.

"Wilkinson, calm down. Use your words," his mother said, sotto voce.

The howling only got louder, and they left the dining room in disgrace.

"He's an active little guy," John said. He looked at me with a sideways glance and closed-lip smile. He sipped coffee and tried not to gloat that it wasn't our kids for a change.

I nibbled my muffin in silence.

Adam, Carole Ann, Maya (seated on Mom's lap), husband John and Nick

Blowing Smoke

by
Pearl Vork-Zambory

There was a time when it was just "The Boy" and me.

Young, poor, inclined to eat breakfast for dinner and drink far too much Kool-Aid—we had it made.

One year, when The Boy was 12, I managed to put away $20 here, $20 there, and come up with a cabin rental on a lake up north—a full week in their last available cabin for the summer. It was nothing fancy, just a small living room, three tiny bedrooms, a bathroom and a kitchen. We had a small boat, with outboard engine available for an additional cost, and a dock just outside the front door.

That June, I packed a dozen books, The Boy packed his cousin Kyle, who was a year younger, and we three made the trip six hours north to the summer vacation cabin. When we arrived, the boys insisted that they sleep on the dock the first night.

"What, so you can roll off it and then I gotta explain to

everyone how I let two kids drown on my watch? No way," was my motherly response.

"What if only one of us drowns?" The Boy countered. "What if Kyle, specifically, is the only one who drowns?"

Significantly smaller than The Boy, Kyle cuffed him on the back of the head. The Boy picked him up and squeezed him until he squeaked.

"You're funny," I said, and yet I was still thinking, *No.*

The rest of the first day was taken up by driving to town for groceries, venturing into the out-of-doors in a swimsuit for the first time that season, and convincing Kyle that even if The Boy did give him a dollar, eating a minnow is disgusting. You know, all the usual.

Around midnight, the kids, reeking of popcorn, went to bed each in a tiny room, after making elaborate plans to capture more minnows in the morning.

It was at 2 A.M. when I heard the whispering and laughing. *Pssss, psss, psss. Hee, hee, hee.*

I hadn't gone to sleep yet, choosing to read for a little bit. I set my book down. *Well, those little . . .*

I slid out of my double bed, bare feet on cold linoleum. Opening my bedroom door, I eased into the dark hallway.

Kyle's room was empty, save for the suitcase that appeared to have exploded in the center of it. The Boy's door was closed. And like so many good women before me, I pressed my ear to it.

Pssss, psss, psss. Hee, hee, hee. And then I heard something that scared me. "And he took the cigarette from his mom's purse and she never even knew!" I pulled away from the door and frowned. *Hmmm.*

I pushed my ear back against the door as The Boy began to whisper. In such low tones, surely this was seditious material. Thoughts flashed in my mind: *Cigarettes first! Now what? Booze? Sex? Drugs? Holy moly, a gang! Is that it? Are the boys going to join a gang?*

"Hey, Kyle."

"What?"

"You know what the greatest thing in the world is?"

"No. What?"

There was the sound of The Boy sucking air into his lungs, blowing it out. *Oh, my baby!* My heart skipped a beat as I pictured him blowing smoke out his bedroom window.

The Boy sighed in exaggerated bliss.

"Mentadent toothpaste. My teeth are so clean. Man that stuff is tight!"

I turned around and went back to bed with a smile on my face. *Toothpaste!* I let them sleep on the dock the next night.

Kyle (left) and The Boy (Dylan)

A Mother's Revenge

by
Julie Royce

There was a little girl, who had a little curl,
Right in the middle of her forehead.
When she was good, she was very good indeed,
but when she was bad she was horrid.

~~ Henry Wadsworth Longfellow (1807-1882)

I sometimes wonder how Longfellow described a little girl who wasn't born until a century after his death. Not only did he know my Courtney, but he knew her well enough to paint her tantrums with poetic precision. Sweet, cuddly and adorable to a fault, my two-year-old daughter was trouble on steroids.

I'm not talking about day-to-day struggles.

"I wear my big coat with the hood to see Dr. Lewak," she said. I had less than a half-hour to be on time for the appointment. It was the middle of August and the temperature soared to 87 stifling degrees.

"I wear my Christmas dress to the park." My mommy sensibilities argued velvet with satin ribbon didn't mix with slides and sandboxes.

"I wear my swimsuit to the grocery store." The rain was 3 degrees short of sleet and I didn't want to be cited for child endangerment.

Neither am I referring to the physical force it took to get rigid little arms into an appropriate outfit without hurting her, nor her lay-down-screaming-and-kicking-on-the-floor rage when I succeeded.

I scoff at typical toddler tantrums, mere fodder for family stories and polite dinnertime conversation. My daughter's *Trifecta of Terror* took the terrible twos to Longfellow's literary *horrid* level. Her near-catastrophes still have the power to raise goose bumps on my forearms. I wonder how either she or I survived until she developed common sense, outgrew her willfulness and left for college.

The first clue that Courtney was more than an average danger to herself came a week after she turned two. I prepared to give her a bath and laid a pair of footed pajamas sporting teddy bears on the vanity.

"I wear my pink, flowered jammies, Mommy."

It wasn't so much a question as it was an order, and since I preferred to let her win battles of little import, I committed the *Cardinal Mommy Sin*. I left the bathroom with Courtney loose and the water running. My daughter trudged after me toward her bedroom, but halfway down the hall she did a quick reverse, beat me to the bathroom and closed the door. No problem—until I heard the sickening, ever-so-faint click that stopped my heart. She had locked me out. I rushed for the phone, dialed 911 and stood on the other side of the barricade that put my daughter a step away from drowning.

"Courtney, honey." I fought the panic in my voice. "Talk to Mommy. Sit down on the floor and I will tell you a story."

"Water, Mommy."

"No, no, sweet girl. We'll play in the water later."

"Once upon a time . . . " I started with "Little Red Riding Hood" and had almost finished "Hansel and Gretel" when the police rang the bell.

"Stay right there," I said, "Mommy will be back in a second." I sprinted downstairs to unlock the door for the rescue crew. In my peripheral vision, I noted water gushing from the base of the dining room chandelier. The carpet sloshed under my feet.

The cops dismantled the bathroom door. I grabbed a naked Courtney, wrapped her in a towel, and then answered a series of questions that suggested the stern police officers had concern that my daughter might not survive the night if she remained in my custody. Finally, convinced there was no need for the immediate removal of my children—Courtney and my seven-year-old son, Jes—from the home, they left. When my heart stopped racing, I contemplated which to do first—give Courtney a bath or clean up the flood precipitated by the tub's plugged overflow valve.

The second incident that caused me to worry that Courtney might not survive to adulthood came one of the many times I banished her to her room. She had thrown a glass of milk on the floor because I wouldn't agree to ice cream instead of a grilled cheese sandwich with apple and carrot sticks for lunch. Incensed that she couldn't choose her menu, she howled. Her face reddened, her eyes bugged out, her breath grew ragged. I scooped her up and carried her upstairs to her bedroom. Using a mother's logic, I sat her on the ruffled spread and said, "You will stay here until you settle down."

"No, Mommy. Ice cream!"

She stormed out of the room after me, kicking at my legs and wailing louder. "Ice cream!" She hadn't forgotten why she screamed and continued on principle.

"Kicking is not allowed," I said.

I returned her to her bedroom then made my exit, shutting the door behind me. I held it closed as I listened to her refrain: "Ice cream! Ice cream. Ice cream . . . " Her demand grew fainter and fainter before it stopped.

In a precursor to today's time-outs, I watched the second hand of my watch tick off two minutes. The bedroom was quiet. I should have been smarter than to leave Courtney anywhere for two full minutes without supervision, even in a childproofed room. I opened the door, saw her and swallowed my shriek so I wouldn't scare her. My daughter had pushed out the screen and sat on a second-story ledge talking to the five-year-old neighbor looking up from the curb across the street.

"OK, Courtney." I put my arms around her before she could tumble to her death, reeled her in, and said, "How about a grilled cheese sandwich *before* the ice cream?"

"No. No grilled cheese. Strawberry ice cream."

At two years old, she had already taught me the finer points of negotiation. "I have an idea," I said. "How about a grilled cheese sandwich and a strawberry milkshake at the same time?" Courtney considered this a victory and agreed. But I, as a mother, knew I had won because I would be serving a nutritious blend of fresh strawberries and skim milk.

A month later, before I had time to regain my equilibrium from the screen-tampering trauma, I experienced the trifecta. My best friend, Jan, offered to pick up my quiet and gentle son Jes for a Saturday afternoon Cub Scout bake sale. My home-baked contribution to the event had to be delivered in the morning. Jan volunteered to drop off my killer chocolate chip-macadamia nut cookies then take the boys to the park. I'd catch up with them after Courtney's nap.

All that cookie baking while watching Courtney had left me no time to shower or dress. My condo had a secluded entryway, not visible to neighbors, so I wasn't too worried what I looked like, wearing nothing but a football jersey that came 6 inches below my butt. I ushered Jes out the front door while carrying the two-dozen cookies, and met Jan as she sauntered up the walkway. I passed off the cookies and turned to step back inside when I heard the sickening slam of the front door. Déjà vu. Locked out again.

I really, really didn't want to call 911, sure that as a repeat offender, the police would be obligated to question my mothering skills with less compassion this time. So I stood outside, aware that the slightest bend or twist or breeze would reveal stuff that no one had a right to see. I was determined to talk my way back into the house.

"Courtney," I said.

"Hi, Mommy."

Good, I thought, *she's close to the door*. "Turn the button on the doorknob so Mommy can get in."

I heard the scratching of little fingers, but nothing happened.

"Can't," came the tiny voice from the other side.

"Yes, honey, you can. Twist the button. Please . . . please . . . puh-leeeeze."

"Can't, Mommy."

"Let Mommy in and she will make you a cup of hot cocoa and read you *Sleeping Beauty*."

"Can't."

I gave up and ran next door. "Call the fire department!" I thought that enlisting help from a different agency might save me from a meeting with Child Protective Services. "Courtney is locked inside—ALONE. Make sure you tell them there is no fire so they don't come with their lights flashing."

The fire department deemed it an emergency. Lights blazed and sirens blared as they pulled to a stop in front of my condo. The crowd of neighbors grew as a uniformed firefighter fumbled with the door. Then he stepped inside and announced, loud enough for the gawking onlookers to hear, "I don't see a child in here." I raced upstairs as I tugged at the bottom of the jersey, hoping the fireman behind me wasn't getting a view that in other circumstances would be judged pornographic. He followed me into my bedroom where Courtney lay on my king-sized bed sucking her thumb and clutching her blankie, the image of a Madonna in the making.

"I'm tired, Mommy," she said.

Two weeks ago, a grown-up Courtney brought her two

sons to my house. Ezra is almost four and is sensitive and easy. Noah is two and is equally precious, but afflicted with his mother's peculiar brand of insanity. We walked to my condo association's clubhouse where the boys love the game room. Noah climbed the castle wall and perched on the high ledge. He looked at his Mommy and announced, "I'm jumping," simultaneous with his leap. Courtney was quick enough to catch him and avoid a crash landing.

"Noah," she cried, "you can't jump unless Mommy is ready to catch you."

A bit shaken, I couldn't suppress the grin that tugged at the corners of my mouth. Perhaps if Longfellow were alive today, he'd write a new poem and title it, "Sweet Revenge."

Two-year-old
Courtney

Parenting 911

by
Lucy James

"Parenting 911?" you ask. "Aren't all parenting diatribes supposed to say 'Parenting 101'?"

Well, I suppose you're right. But basic, beginning parenting issues can be a bit boring. How much is there, really, to discuss? Babies eat, sleep, cry, sleep, poop and sleep. Then they sleep some more. How hard can that be? Sure, there are questions about bottle or breast, crib or family bed and cloth or disposable diapers. But all that, if you'll pardon the pun, is kids' stuff. Despite what you read in some magazines, there is more to parenting than potty training.

When I was pregnant with my son, I was constantly tired. My daughter had just celebrated her first birthday and she was a handful by herself. Add a pregnancy to the mix and I was a very worn-out gal.

One day when my husband had a day off from work, I told him how tired I had been and how tired I remained no matter how much sleep I got at night. He graciously offered to watch our daughter while I took a nap. And I innocently thanked him for his thoughtfulness.

Half an hour later, my husband said, "Honey, wake up. You really need to get up now."

My daughter was barely tall enough to see over the edge of the bed. She got as close as she could to my face and said, "Hi, Mama."

When the word "hi" literally blew out of her mouth, I instantly recognized the odor. It was kerosene. I bolted upright and screamed at my husband, trying to find out what had happened. He came in and explained that a small amount of kerosene had been left in a cup on the kitchen floor next to the wood stove. We frequently used a touch of kerosene to jump-start the fire. My daughter had found the cup and deciding she was thirsty, she drank the contents—she drank kerosene! I immediately called Poison Control. They asked me if she had vomited. I told them she hadn't, but I could make her vomit. They told me that as long as she hadn't vomited, she was OK. I learned that kerosene is dangerous only when, or if, it enters the lungs during vomiting, not during swallowing. They told me to watch her for about an hour and monitor her breathing. I did as I was told and she seemed to be fine. An hour later, Poison Control called me back to find out if she was still feeling OK. I told them she was and they told me that the worst was over.

When my son first learned to walk, he loved to carry things, just because he could. That's when I learned that toenails can be lost under the most innocent of circumstances.

He began to get things for himself instead of waiting for me to get them for him. At about 18 months old, my son decided he wanted a cup of orange juice. Instead of bringing me the empty cup to fill, he walked into the kitchen and picked up a 64-ounce can of Donald Duck orange juice. He had taken only five or six steps when he dropped the can on his big toe. Fearing a broken bone, my husband and I took him to the emergency room for X-rays. All bones were intact, but the toenail was barely hanging on.

The nail wobbled around for a few days before it finally gave up the ghost. The new nail finally started to emerge. It had grown out about halfway when my son got thirsty again. Another can of Donald Duck and another injured toe. We skipped the ER on this one and just sat around waiting for the nail to fall off again. I learned that we either needed to get to the juice before our son did or to buy smaller cans.

Not long after the string of toenail incidents, we experienced another home accident. I was in the kitchen cooking dinner. My husband was in the living room watching TV. My daughter was in the bathroom, and my two-and-a-half-year-old son was playing in the hallway. As I flipped the hamburgers in the skillet, I heard my son let out a blood-curdling scream.

I ran down the hall as fast as I could, but didn't see him anywhere. He was in my bedroom, just sitting on the floor. He looked up at me, not making a noise, and I wondered what all the screaming had been about. Then I saw it. One of my mother-in-law's hairpins was sticking out of the electrical outlet. I screamed for my husband to come in and remove it. I picked up my son and held him close. I kept asking him if he was OK. I couldn't believe he was acting like nothing had happened. My husband came in and looked at the hairpin. And then looked at it some more. While he stood there trying to remember which breaker worked the bedroom, I smelled something burning. My panic kicked into severe overdrive.

"Turn off the main breaker!" I screamed. "The wiring in the wall is on fire!"

My husband kicked off the main breaker and the house went black. We fixed the situation with the outlet, but we still didn't know what to do with our child.

My husband said, "Call Granny. She'll know what to do."

I ran to the phone to make the call, but the cordless phone doesn't work without electricity. So I clutched my son tightly and ran to Granny's house. She lived just behind us, so it really wasn't that far to go.

I got to the door and pounded loudly. She wasn't home, but I made an important discovery standing on her doorstep—I still smelled something burning. Then I had a horrible revelation. The house was not burning, my son was! The smell was my son's scorched flesh. The palm of his hand and all five fingers were badly burned.

I ran back to the house and showed my husband our son's hand. He grabbed the car keys and we headed for the hospital. I didn't even put my son in his car seat. I held him in my lap to monitor his breathing.

We got to the hospital in record time. The nurses raced him into an exam room and immediately hooked him up to heart monitors. They eventually found out that he hadn't suffered any more damage than his burned hand.

More adventures followed when my daughter was around age six and my son was four. They asked me to buy them a sandbox. I thought about their request—for about two seconds. Then I told them, "No." They whined, begged and pleaded, but I stood firm. I could not, in good conscience, buy my children a box of dirt to play in, knowing that said dirt would soon make its way to my carpet, not to mention dealing with the laundry and extra baths!

The kids still whined about my decision, but they got over it in a few days. Or, so I thought. They were playing in my bedroom the next week and I went to check on them. They were being very quiet and experience told me that something was amiss.

They were sitting on my bed playing. I was happy they were being so good to each other. Then I stepped further into the room. My bed was covered in Parmesan cheese. They had swiped a can of the powdered cheese from the refrigerator and squirreled it away to the bedroom. They then proceeded to pour the entire contents on my bed. They played in the cheese bed, as if it were a sandbox.

I ranted and raved to no end. I threatened horrible punishments that would last their entire lives. They pretended to be afraid and repentant. I chased them away and they retreated to their rooms to avoid my wrath. I opened the bedroom window and shook out the sheet, blankets and pillows. The cheese seemed to multiply.

Two days later, my children were in my bedroom, again being very quiet. I slowly and dreadfully plodded down the hall. There they sat on my bed playing in a mound of salt. Having utilized all of the Parmesan cheese, they decided to use a box of salt as a creative alternative.

We went through the whole scene again. I ranted and threatened and they bowed their heads and looked like they were sorry. I cleaned the mess and ran out of clean linens in the process.

After these incidents, I was thinking twice about Parenting 911. Maybe they should have offered a class and called it just that. And maybe there I would have learned that buying my kids a sandbox would have been a good investment after all, for both their enjoyment and my sanity.

Always a Kid

by
Ken McKowen

My wife accuses me of not being your typical stepparent. Actually, she has teased me about being more of a "step sibling" to her two children. It's because I'm a true kid at heart.

I've known both of her children even before they were born. The two of us, at the time married to different people, were business partners before she became pregnant with her first child and during her second pregnancy, as well. It wasn't until late 2000, when her daughter was eight and her son three, that she divorced. We were married in June 2002.

When the kids were much younger, I never saw a problem running through our home, playing silly and very raucous rounds of tag or having all-out Nerf sponge dart wars. We'd have fart and silly-face contests, run around the backyard chasing each other with the hose going full blast and, many times, we'd see who could eat the most ice cream.

During our many family trips, it was a given that the three

of us would have an all-out pillow fight in the hotel room while my wife tried to keep us from getting too out of control. One classic kid trip was when we stayed overnight on the Queen Mary in Long Beach, California. I had the youngest stepchild—Shawn—convinced that the historic ship was haunted, and I ran up and down the very long hallways in sheets from our hotel room bed, pretending to be a ghost.

When Shawn was about four years old, we saw the movie *Twins* starring Danny DeVito and Arnold Schwarzenegger—back in his pre-governor days. In one of the many hilarious scenes, Arnold picks up a car, something Shawn found absolutely amazing. He figured anyone who could lift a car had to be incredibly strong. I said I was strong, too, striking poses and flexing my muscles for him. Shawn scoffed, in his own charming way, at the thought that I could be as powerful and strong as Arnold.

One afternoon, we were heading out on an errand. My wife and the kids got into the car first while I helped Shawn into his car seat. After I buckled him in and closed his door, I reached down and grabbed the bottom of the car, grunted very loudly and began rocking the car up and down on its shocks. This trick instantly gave Shawn the impression I was actually lifting the car, à la Arnold Schwarzenegger. The surprise and amazement on Shawn's face that his old stepdad could actually lift a car was priceless. Over the next week or two, I repeated my super-strength trick many times, always to Shawn's approval and amusement.

A few weeks later, we stopped at a local fast-food Mexican restaurant for dinner. Shawn loved dropping quarters into what used to be penny gumball machines, many of which now dispense those little golf ball-sized clear plastic containers that hold non-edible prizes like plastic figurines and tattoos. But our family rule was that he had to eat all his dinner before getting two quarters for the machines.

Shawn raced through his meal and after showing me everything was gone—including nearly every speck of food on his plate, I gave him two quarters. Money in hand, he made a beeline to the machines. There were several to choose from, so he stood there for a few minutes, thoughtfully and carefully weighing his options. Finally, he selected one that promised a miniature ninja warrior figurine.

When the plastic container dropped through the machine's chute, Shawn was on cloud nine. He grabbed his treasure and immediately ran back to our table, telling us all about how he came to his decision. Then with all the excitement his little four-year-old body could handle, he attempted to open the container. If you've seen these containers before, you know they are made of two halves designed to unsnap and release their bounty. The key word is "designed," because there is nothing easy about opening these small containers.

Frustrated, Shawn finally gave up and handed it to me. "Here, Dad. Will you open this for me, please?"

I took the clear plastic container and with the confidence that would have made Arnold proud, I twisted, squeezed, twisted some more, pinched, thumped and twisted harder, to no avail. It refused to open. As I sat sweating and obviously struggling, the original smile of anticipation on Shawn's face began to fade.

Finally, I gave up, at least momentarily, but not before Shawn looked up at me, completely heartbroken, and said, "Dad, what's wrong? You used to be strong."

I sat there, stunned. Then I started laughing. The rest of the family joined me, and our laughter grew louder as we looked at Shawn. The poor boy just stood there, mouth agape, not understanding what was so funny. It was then I explained my car trick and the fact that I wasn't as strong as Arnold Schwarzenegger. He was not happy that the joke had been on him, but after a few seconds, he relented and joined in the laughter. Once I had regained my composure, I opened the plastic container, but not before my superhuman façade had been significantly deflated in my stepson's eyes.

Twelve years later, I'm still a goofy kid. Shawn and I have a great relationship and I'm so proud to be his friend and stepfather. While I may have lost my super strength, I don't ever anticipate losing my childlike enthusiasm for having fun.

Ken goofing around with four-year-old Shawn on the beach, and then 12 years later, the two at an Oregon blueberry farm

I'm Not Telling!

by
Elizabeth Sandahl

When my son Lee turned 11, he was old enough that, legally, he did not need a sitter after school to keep an eye on him. He assured me that he could take care of himself just fine. Sometimes, as a single parent trying to work and raise a child, I believed what I wanted to believe. Such was the case here.

I had recently finished business college and worked at a bank until 5:30 P.M., and it didn't take long for me to get home after work. Lee got home from school about 4 P.M., and convinced me that he would be OK on his own until I got home. *What could go wrong in two hours?* I asked myself.

Around that time, Lee begged for an allowance. He could not do many things to earn money, so I worked out a deal that I would pay him $2 an hour allowance on the days I worked. While $4 a day does not sound like much, $20 a week sounded to me like a great allowance for an 11-year-old boy. *I would have to pay that much to a sitter for those two hours a day anyway,* I reasoned. I put one stipulation on the deal and he agreed to it: If he didn't do his chores before I got home, I would deduct money from his daily earnings.

I worked in the back office of the bank, and my supervisors, knowing Lee was home alone, allowed him to call me when he got home from school. Sometimes he would ask to go play with a neighbor friend after school. He was first supposed to do whatever chore I had assigned, but knowing little boys, I am sure he played first, and then dashed home to get the chore finished before I pulled into the driveway.

If Lee wanted to go somewhere or do something I did not agree to, he would get mad and hang up the phone. And he hung up the phone a lot! When I would call back, he wouldn't answer. Oh, I would get so frustrated with him! There I was, trying to earn a living, and he was not making it easy. You can imagine what would happen then; I would be angry at my son while I was working, but I could not leave. Of course he would get a chewing out when I got home, because I was still mad when I got there. When Lee's phone calls made me angry, my co-workers, with knowing looks on their faces, always asked, "What did Lee do now?"

Often, Lee would call and tell me, "You are going to be mad when you get home, but I am not going to tell you what I did!" Then he would hang up the phone. I wasn't just mad at him once I got home, I was mad while I was still at work! The ladies in the back office thought it was hilarious. I think they looked forward to Lee's daily call. I, on the other hand, didn't think it was funny at all.

In the garage, I stored a china hutch I had bought at a

sale-barn auction. I refinished the hutch by stripping off all of the blackish varnish and putting on a coat of clear Varathane. It was a nice hutch with glass doors and three glass shelves. After I had refinished it, I took it into the house. I tried it in the family room, the living room, the dining room and the hallway before I came to the conclusion that it didn't fit anywhere with my other furnishings. I finally decided to sell it by putting an ad in the newspaper.

Also stored in our garage were my other son Mike's motorcycle and his Chevy Blazer. Mike was in Germany while in the Army and I was storing his toys for him. The Blazer was not new, but the motorcycle had less than 200 miles on it.

One day, I got a call at work from Lee, with his usual warning about my being mad when I got home. Then he hung up the phone. I won't write the thoughts that went through my mind, but I'll bet anyone who saw me could have guessed. The girls in the office stopped what they were doing and turned to watch my red-faced reaction.

When I got home, Lee was right. I was mad . . . really mad! He had taken one of his buddies, who was not supposed to be in the house when I was not home, out to the garage. This action was a technicality that my son figured out to keep from breaking my "no house" rule.

Showing off that he could climb on his brother's motorcycle, up he went. Then down he and the motorcycle crashed! The bike bumped the hutch, which in turn knocked all three shelves down into the bottom, shattering the glass. The turn signal and clutch handle on the motorcycle broke. Fortunately, the rest of the motorcycle was unscathed, and so was my son.

When I got home, I had a loud conversation with Lee and I informed him that he would have to pay for all of the damage out of his allowance. Since I am a mom and I love my son—or maybe because I didn't want to listen to him beg constantly for money—I only took half of his allowance at a time. I had several calls about the hutch that evening in response to my ad. No one wanted to buy it with broken shelves, not even if I would deduct the price of new shelves. It cost me $30 for new plate-glass shelves and I ended up trading the hutch to a friend for something I wanted.

It was several months before Lee got to keep all the allowance he earned. I made him reimburse me for every dollar I paid out. Plus, his brother was not pleased with him, and I am sure he called him a couple of names when Lee talked to him on the phone. I wonder if Lee hung up on him, too!

One weekend, I repainted the living room and dining room a light mint green, and it looked nice. I came home from work one day and sat at the dining room table. The way the light hit the wall, I noticed a dent in the sheetrock. It looked like a footprint. I casually got up and walked into the family room where Lee was watching TV. I reached down and picked up one of his tennis shoes, turned around and headed back to the dining room. That got his attention in a hurry. When I took the shoe to the dining room, I placed the front part of the sole into the dent. *Gee, a perfect fit! Imagine that!* Since I had caught him red-footed, he had to admit he had kicked the wall when he was angry. He had not called me about that incident. We had another loud discussion before I doled out his punishment.

Eventually, I hated to go to work. Every day someone said, "What did Lee do yesterday, Liz? Your life is just like a soap opera." And it was. As little boys go, Lee was not a bad kid, but he did keep life both interesting and frustrating at the same time. Whenever he said, "I'm not telling," there was no telling what he had done.

Lee with Cassie

World War IV

by
Sarah L. Johnson

You might wonder why I call this story "World War IV." It's because of the day my four-year-old declared war in the midst of a play date. He became disgruntled when, despite his objections, his female playmate insisted on looking at him. He scuttled to my side, whining incoherently over the violation of his inalienable right to not be looked at. Call it reflex or schadenfreude—a German term for "pleasure derived from the misfortune of others"—but I laughed.

His reaction: shocked silence.

It actually shut him up. For a brief pinch of time, I thought I'd discovered the key to all the parenting doors. Then he opened his mouth. The sound was extraordinary, like a dozen sets of vocal cords howling the anthem of hell. I had unknowingly launched WWIV. I looked to the mother of the little girl. She shrugged. At a loss, I scraped my son off the floor and deposited him in his room.

After 10 minutes of crashing and bellowing, the noise abruptly ceased. I opened the door. Evidence of his squall was everywhere: dumped out toys, emptied dresser, mattress pulled off the bed. The very air was electric, but there was no sign of life. Then the mattress heaved. A red-faced goblin scurried out from underneath.

I expected anger. Instead, I was greeted with wide tear-filled eyes. Small and vulnerable he reached out with skinny arms that had recently been so soft and plump.

Then I made a critical error. It is shockingly easy to be seduced by a child's affections, to believe that you are meeting in a neutral zone of hugs and cuddles. But when such a meeting occurs in the midst of chaos, be wary. Remember that the child cares nothing for traditional rules of engagement and neither should you.

In this case, I forgot rule number one: "The child is the enemy." The walls surrounding my heart crumbled. I held my son and buried my face in his neck, noting his dire need for a bath. In a gentle voice, I asked if he would please pick up his toys for Mama.

Hell chorus: redux, I thought. My simple request sent him into another raging counterstrike. He dug in his heels and wasn't going to give up any ground. Further attempts to negotiate with the creature were met with flailing limbs and gnashing teeth. I'd abandoned my guests. My coffee was cold. The play date was history. And I was chasing my tail.

Finally, I screamed at him. I screamed at him to stop screaming.

A note on perspective: towering over your enemy does

not mean you have the higher ground. Rule number two: "Pride can level entire civilizations." Blinded by my pride, I'd allowed the creature to goad me into a tantrum of my very own. No doubt it was deliberate. His smirk signified a perfect understanding of mutually assured destruction. *Well played, little one.*

"This isn't over," I said, backing out of his room.

He slammed the door in my face.

I dashed downstairs to regroup. Fortunately, my friend and her daughter were content to wait it out and provide moral support from the home front. I redeployed to the combat zone.

He'd been busy. The mattress was back on the bed, but he had ripped the plastic cover of the cold air return off the wall and shoved a pillow into the duct. The creature huddled under his blanket.

Ceasefires are always tenuous and must be handled with care. I had no idea that the little girl had followed me to the front line. She swerved around my legs and yanked the blanket off my son. I clapped my hand over my mouth. The little girl squealed. The four-year-old creature roared. He'd taken it to the next level, much like The Incredible Hulk, except instead of a missing shirt, he was entirely bottomless—pants, underwear, everything.

He scrambled off his bed and shuffled in a wide circle, searching for cover while commanding the little girl to, "Geddout! Geddout! GEDDOUT!"

I tried to control myself, but there was just no way. My unbridled laughter filled the ruined room. The creature screeched loudly enough to make the windows quake. The little girl fled.

Still laughing, I tugged the pillow out of the duct and prepared to let the hammer fall.

"Looking for these?" I plucked the Spiderman briefs from the duct and shook them in front of his face. "Un-der-pants!"

He gawped at me. The third rule, "All ethics are situational," had thrown him completely. He opened his mouth. The beginnings of that awful scream emerged. Then the sound rippled into a hesitant, broken laugh.

The atmosphere depolarized in a snap. He grunted and giggled and finally succumbed to that gut-shaking, knee-buckling laugh unique to small children. He crawled into my lap and together we lost our minds. No dignity, no pride, no pants.

There are no easy choices in time of war. A child humiliated is nothing to take pleasure in. On that day, however, my son learned that I will burn down his world, and mine, and salt the earth before I will surrender. An important lesson for him, but I learned something, too. It's one of the few things I know for sure, and I'll leave it with you now.

Laughter is a vector of contagion, joy gone viral. Once infected, we're truly on neutral ground—clutching our bellies and kicking our heels in the air.

CHAPTER
SEVEN

All Grown Up

Been there, done that.

The Pussy Riot

by
Kari Lynn Collins

Yeah, you read that right.

Last Wednesday, I drove my grown son, Tom, to the Oklahoma City airport and said goodbye as he left for his new home—and new life—as a grad student in Boston.

I'm not sure, but I think he bought my excuse when I told him my eyes were watering due to an unfortunate accident with tear gas and shampoo that morning. At any rate, he made it to Boston unscathed and I stopped crying about an hour later.

I raised my children in a small town where they could get gas for their car at the local convenience store when they were in high school and tell the clerk I'd be in to pay for it tomorrow. The clerk would say OK. It was a simple, comfortable upbringing.

When Tom told me he'd gotten an offer he couldn't refuse from the University of Massachusetts Boston, I began to realize that the time had come for me to be his personal pantywaist. At 6-feet tall and just over 200 pounds, Tom was an offensive lineman and competitive power lifter in high school, so he could take care of himself. But it's my job as a mother to worry about things that will most likely never happen. And, to be unreasonably upset when I think someone has hit him in the head, stolen his cellphone and started answering my texts.

But I'm getting ahead of myself.

Tom and I had been communicating quite a lot Wednesday, Thursday and Friday, me trying to help him get settled in, cross-country. Or more likely, him letting me feel like I was still needed.

I hadn't heard from him at all Saturday, so around 10 A.M., I called him. Voice mail. Called him again at 11:30. Voice mail. Finally, 2 P.M rolled around and I decided that I would make him talk to me using his favorite form of communication.

So I texted him.

Me: "Hey Bub, you OK?"

And finally, a sign of life.

Tom: "Yeah, I'm volunteering at a Pussy Riot benefit put on by a punk feminist organization and can't talk right now. Literally."

What? Really?! I screamed to myself. What son would text his mother a message like that and not think she would have scenarios in her head of his abduction and the kidnappers toying with her emotions via text message?

Me: "I have no idea what you're talking about. Who are you and where is my son? Is this Tom?"

Tom: "Yep. Google 'pussy riot.'"

To be fair, Tom thinks Googling is the quickest answer for most everything. Most kidnappers wouldn't know that. I took my finger off the Boston Police phone number I had on speed-dial.

I followed the potential kidnapper's instructions and Googled "pussy riot." I did this even though I knew in my heart that my email's inbox would now be flooded with SPAM of the most hideous variety. I love my boy that much.

Turns out in February three women in Russia sang an anti-Vladimir Putin song on the steps of a church, and after Putin was elected in March, they were all arrested for—get this—hooliganism. (Side note: If I am ever arrested for anything in my life, I hope it is this, because in the United States that usually means overnight in the drunk tank, AND I will have the charge of *hooliganism* on my permanent life record.)

Not so in Russia.

All of the women remain in jail, and the Boston Pussy Riot was an all-day concert and vegan barbecue to raise money for their legal defense fund. Apparently, the Russian girls' punishment carried the possibility of up to seven years in prison and removal of their parental rights, even though free speech is a guaranteed right in the Russian constitution.

Me: "Found it. Holy shit!"

Tom: "Right? I'm grilling zucchini in pussy riot solidarity."

Me: "Are you going vegan as well?"

Tom: "F_ _k no."

I love it. My son has a conscience and a love for good corn-fed beef. He'll be just fine.

Mom's cell phone text message

Almost on the Six O'clock News

by
Pam Young

It was such a scorching dog day in late August that the birds were hot-tubbing in our backyard birdbath. I was wearing my bathing suit and had turned the air-conditioning down another notch despite the *green* voice in my head that said, *You should be ashamed*. It didn't help my mood to think about my daughter Peggy, her husband Tyler and my two young grandchildren, Jacob and Sophie, working outside in 100-degree weather at a camp for foster children in our community. I admired their compassion and magnanimity to devote an entire summer running the camp and I was glad they were due home that evening.

I glanced across the room at my husband, who was engrossed in his book. "I feel guilty," I told him.

"Why?" he asked not looking up.

"Oh, I don't know. I wish I'd gone out to the camp more than twice this summer. Maybe I should've stayed a few nights and helped with the campers."

"You don't camp."

"I know but . . . "

"You would have been miserable." He put the book down. "I think your words were, 'Camping's like going out in the woods and pretending you're homeless,'" he said, trying to sound like a woman.

"OK, right, but I should've done something to help them."

"You wanna invite 'em over?"

"No, they'll be too tired. I wish I'd done something at their house to make them scream when they walk through their front door tonight, like people do on those home-make-over programs."

"Honey, it's noon, don't start thinking about remodeling or painting anything. There's no time."

Time. Darn, why hadn't I thought of this yesterday?

Deep in thought, I went to the fridge to make something for our lunch. I found an empty cheese wrapper, a tablespoon of tuna and three cherry tomatoes. I needed groceries and that's when it hit me. I would zip over to Cram-co (that's what we call Costco because we end up cramming our car to the ceiling with every visit) and fill one of those 18-wheeler-sized carts with every treat I could find. I'd stock up Peggy's fridge, cupboard and freezer with meals and snacks to last a month. Jumbo-sized Pringles and ranch dip and chocolate chip muffins would absolutely thrill their junk-food-deprived systems.

I could hardly contain my excitement—kind of like those

women on the free shopping sprees sprinting for the boneless hams and steaks when the bell goes off. Buying groceries for someone else is so much more fun than buying for yourself! With each item I tossed in the cart, I knew I was escalating the reaction factor. They'd fling open the refrigerator and freezer to discover a Sears Kenmore commercial.

My trunk stuffed with groceries, I pulled up in front of the house and froze. There was a strange blue car in the driveway. Just as I was about to dig out my cell phone—which was wedged between two frozen cheesecakes—and report the intruder to the sheriff, I remembered a 20-year-old female relative had agreed to housesit while they were away. I'd also got wind of a boyfriend joining her from time to time—probably meaning night to night—and I *wasn't* real happy about that. But I reminded myself it was none of my business and I would be pleasant and friendly . . . this was a mission of fun!

I popped out of the car, opened the trunk and scooped up an armload of goodies. Sprinting up the walk and kicking open the unlocked front door, I headed to the kitchen and caught sight of a huge young man in boxers and an undershirt coming down the hall from the bedroom.

"WHO ARE YOU?!" he bellowed.

"WHO ARE YOU?!" I bellowed back.

"I'm Dennis Gilbert." Silent pause. "And I am going to ask you one more time, WHO ARE YOU?"

By now I was really steaming!

"I'm Pam Young!" I spit back, my body puffing up like a cat that was ready to fight. "Peggy Carlson's *mother*!"

Dennis had a change in demeanor—he seemed to kind

of shrink back from his attack-mode stance as his brain ran a make on the situation.

Hah! You better watch it, buddy, I proudly thought to myself. *You're in big trouble now!*

"Oh, Peggy Carlson," he uttered. "Uh, she lives next door." His hand gestured to the right.

I know, I could have been shot that hot summer afternoon, but in my defense, the Carlson home was one of at least a hundred IDENTICAL homes in the subdivision. They all have a maple tree in the SAME spot in the front yard. They all have the SAME hedge between each parcel and they all have the SAME floor plan.

Part of me wanted to ask Dennis, "Could you just not tell Peggy and Tyler this happened?" Then I'd go home and take the food with me. But I knew they'd find out and a bigger part of me needed to get on with making their refrigerator look like a Sears commercial. Besides, I was very grateful I had escaped the six o'clock news.

Pam in Austria, as far away from news crews as possible!

Crying in the Chapel

by
Janet Sheppard Kelleher

My children learned early on that things weren't necessarily bad just because Mom cried. In fact, the situation was often very good. Weddings, anniversaries, graduations, baptisms, birthdays and retirements created just as many heartfelt gully washers as did funerals. The kids thought it was a hoot and made fun of "Mom's happy tears."

My oldest child, David, despised swimming lessons ever since someone at camp told him a person could drown with a teaspoon of water in his lungs. He hated the dead-man's float—he panicked holding his breath for such a long time. Treading water was the worst. Therefore, I insisted that my son master a certain level in swimming before we installed a pool, quoting him the ne'er-believed refrain of every parent, "You'll thank me one day."

"This hurts me worse than it does you," was another adage I would share with my son. And I made him take the swim lessons—

no getting out of them. I watched David advance from pol-
lywog to guppy to minnow to fish. At his birthday swim party,
my tearful day arrived when he paused at the end of the diving
board and mouthed in my direction, "Thanks, Mom."

I required my daughter, Sarah, to take voice lessons to im-
prove the skills she'd learned in chorus. Gifted but lazy, she
hated practicing scales. I told her the hard work would pay off.
Then during an audition for the part of Dorothy in *The Wizard of Oz*, the sound of Sarah's voice singing *Over the Rainbow*
was so perfect and sweet that it melted not only my heart to
tears, but her daddy's, too.

Our last child, Julia, had a mild language problem at
an early age. She couldn't properly ask or answer a question.
Something wasn't synapsing. A speech therapist told us she
needed professional help to overcome this handicap. We
couldn't afford a professional, so I spent the better part of a
year drilling her with question and answer techniques. The day
she spontaneously asked me the first question that made sense,
we were in the car. My tear ducts went wild. I pulled the car off
the road until I could see again, while trying to convince Julia
that she had done nothing wrong, but everything right!

Whenever I feel a familiar flush in the region of my heart,
my face prunes up, my eyes gush and I often cry audibly. I look
around and see other people beaming with pride, while I'm
wailing like a banshee. Since my kids made quite a bit of sport
of me during those times, I told the little scoffers, "What goes
around comes around." I'm happy to say I've been a witness to
some of those special moments.

David married a bit later in life. Thirty is old for a

Southern boy, right? Anyway, during the shortest wedding I've ever witnessed, my son cried so hard I wanted to rush to the altar and wrap my arms around him. Mainly, I wanted him to tell me the reason for his emotion—but we knew.

Sarah is a movie buff. She and I curled up on the sofa one day and watched *The Other Sister*. During the triumphant scene when the marching band played *Seventy-Six Trombones* and the mentally challenged groom shouted, "This is a gift for my bride!" Sarah broke into loud uncontrollable boo-hoos. I wanted to comfort her and have her tell me where those tears came from—but we knew.

Julia taught her preschool class how to sing. Later, a proud parent gave her a professional CD of the class singing a cappella. It was pitch-perfect and as lovely as a chorus of angels. You should have seen the tears in Julia's eyes, which spoke of the pride in her students' accomplishment, when she played the CD for me. I wanted her to admit why she was crying—but we knew.

Tears are oddly appropriate at times. Words are inadequate when our cups run over, so our hearts must do the speaking. They testify by opening the floodgates to the windows of the soul. And in this family, our windows are always open.

If you happen to be walking by a beautiful lawn graduation or garden wedding someday and hear a great caterwauling commotion, that will be me—or one of my kids—happy as can be.

The Practice Run

by
Linda A. Lohman

Some people are just naturally good at the parenting thing. I think my son, Castro, now in his 40s, is one of them. And Castro has two absolutely wonderful children—Ellen and Billy.

I divorced when Castro was eight years old. I always wondered if the lack of a significant male role model in his life would affect his parenting. Apparently not.

Castro creates designer Halloween pumpkins, always makes awesome hot chocolate on game nights and pops his popcorn the old-fashioned way—and with butter. He attends soccer games and taekwondo lessons. He relishes play dates as much as the kids. In fact, he was all excited about ordering a special sled from Germany for the family.

The sled was more like a luge. Just over a yard long, it was about a foot wide and made of solid ash with stainless steel. It was never going to rust or corrode, and even though it weighed only 10 pounds, it had all kinds of steering capabilities. The wood slat seating proved to be a challenge to fit three people aboard, but the straight runners and steering apparatus would be perfect for the family.

I remember the first sled run very well. I was there and witnessed the entire series of events.

Ellen was about eight years old. She had on a bright red cap covering her ears, but no mittens or gloves to keep her hands from becoming frostbitten. Billy was just four. He had on goggles, a hat, gloves and boots.

"OK," Castro said, "here is what we're going to do. We're going to tackle this run. There are no skiers or snowboards allowed. It's 1,500 feet straight down. We are liable to become airborne, so hold on tight. If you fall out, you'll have to walk all the way down. Are you ready?"

"Yes," both kids chimed. They screamed with excitement, cheeks pink and eyes sparkling with the glow of snow.

Billy sat in front. He scrunched up his knees under his chin and grasped the side handles. Ellen sat in the middle. Her legs went around her brother and she gripped him as tightly with her legs as she did the wooden slats she used as handrails. Castro sat aft. He gave a push and ran alongside the sled, screaming, "Don't leave without me! Let me in!"

Billy and Ellen giggled and shrieked, "Go faster!"

Castro made a last lunge and jumped aboard. His long legs encircled the three of them. He yelled, "Look out for the tree! Billy, steer around the tree!"

Billy and Ellen giggled so loudly the tree should have shook! Fortunately, they cleared the tree before coming to a slight dip. Then they were airborne.

"We'll come down hard. Hang on tight!" Castro screamed.

Billy giggled and would have fallen out of the sled were Ellen not holding him so tightly with her legs. At once, she started giggling, too.

"Hang on!"

Another hundred feet and Castro again yelled, "Look out! There's a skier ahead! Skiers are not supposed to be out here! Can we steer around him?"

More screams and yells sounded like at least 15 kids aboard that sled.

A dog loomed in front of the sled. All three of them yelled for her to move and she sauntered off as though she dodged sleds every day.

At some point, Billy lost his hat. The dog was last seen with it, but that didn't slow the trio down.

On and on they careened down the hill. Ellen soon had the hang of it and threw her hands into the air much as she would on a roller coaster.

"Look, Dad—no hands!" she yelled.

"Hang on!" Castro yelled back. He tipped the sled slightly to the side and all fell out onto the rug. Yes, the living room rug.

Lucy, the family's Australian Shepherd, jumped into Billy's lap and dropped the wayward hat. Billy, clad only in his pajamas along with his requisite gear, wanted to celebrate the practice run with hot chocolate. After all, sled rides are cold!

My son is a great parent. He will do anything for his kids, including creating a winter wonderland in the middle of his living room. The shrieks, giggles and ultimate crash that I witnessed that day proved to me that I never needed to worry about my son lacking a role model. All the role models he ever needed were the two sharing his magical sled.

Moonshine and Moonlight

by
Pat Nelson

When my son Steve graduated from high school, my husband, Bob, and I had been dating for just a short time. We invited my son to go to Puerto Vallarta with us, along with another couple. Steve was excited to travel to Mexico for the first time, and also excited to be going to a country where he could legally drink alcohol.

We rented a villa high on the hill overlooking old town Puerto Vallarta. Cooled by a mild breeze, we could see the hot sandy beach and the crashing surf a few miles to the west while parasailers floated in the sky above the ocean.

Steve had his first taste of living on his own. He got to sleep in a small apartment a steep 55-step climb up from our spacious two-bedroom villa.

Steve led us up to his temporary home. My legs burned at the halfway point and I had to rest. Palm trees and tropical flowers lined the stairway. "You won't want to walk home after drinking," I warned him. Finally at the top, we marveled at the view from his open-air living room. The apartment held everything he needed: besides the living room with a view, there was a bedroom with a queen-sized bed, a refrigerator, and a bathroom with a shower.

We all enjoyed the sights and the sun of Mexico. One day, we visited Chico's Paradise, a restaurant perched on granite and overlooking the Horcones River south of town. Children played in the water below the restaurant and stretched their arms toward us, shouting "Peso! Peso!" We tossed pesos and small toys to the children. Other kids dove from the steep rocks and were rewarded with coins.

Steve joined the fun in the river by sliding over a waterfall into a pool of clear water. Once his feet touched the sandy bottom, he swam to shore, climbed up the boulders and did it again. He'd had a couple beers, but was not intoxicated. His mother, on the other hand (yes, that's me!) had just one margarita and turned into the life of the party. "Salud," I said, raising my salt-rimmed glass to tap his beer glass. I was sure I could go down the waterfall, but my son finally convinced me that if I made it down the waterfall, I would never get back up the smooth granite boulders.

That one drink hit me hard. Unbeknownst to me, I had been one of the chosen ones to be served a special tequila. Suddenly, I was as tipsy as the inebriated lady I'd chuckled about at a table across the way. Whew! I didn't know at the time that some guests were served a moonshine tequila that packed quite a kick. To my son's embarrassment, I visited the small souvenir shop and happily bounced off shelves and displays.

He hurriedly got me out of there.

One evening back at the villa, we invited some new friends over for cocktails. My son had a few too many then stumbled up the hill to his *apartamento*. The evening was perfect, with not a cloud in the sky. Bob and I slept in our room with the doors open to the deck, a view of the city lights below and the stars above.

Steve got up late the next morning, slowed by the drinks of the night before. I walked up to his place to see when he was coming down to join us. He slouched on the sofa, hair ruffled from sleep. "Did you hear the storm?" he asked. "The thunder was so loud. And I heard God talk to me."

I snickered. "I didn't hear any thunder. Or God."

I went back down the stairs, deciding to play along with Steve's belief that there had been a big storm. "Terry, Sam," I said to the owners of the villa who lived on the floor above the one we occupied, "Steve thinks there was a huge storm last night, with thunder, but I think he was just hearing the effects of all the beer he drank. He even thought he heard God talk to him. Play along and ask him if he heard the thunder."

"Will do," replied Terry. "And when the wind blows through the palms, it does sometimes sound like voices."

At last, Steve slowly made his way down the stairs. "Hey Steve, that was quite a storm last night, wasn't it?!" said Terry. "Thunder and everything! Did it wake you?"

"See, Mom," said Steve. "I told you."

Steve was more careful about how much he drank after that night, perhaps because of something God had whispered to him through the palms.

A few years later, I invited my daughter Susan to travel to Puerto Vallarta with me. It was just the two of us. Like her brother, she had never been to Mexico. We were there at Halloween, and we took masks, candy and toys to the kids at Chico's Paradise. We sat on the smooth hot rocks above the river and taught the kids to knock on my swim bag, as if it were a door, and say "Trick or Treat." Kids danced around us in Halloween masks that could not hide their big grins, some partially hidden by the masks.

Later, Susan swam while I plunged over the waterfall. We both climbed the granite rocks with the help of a strong rope and several village children.

One evening, we went for the dinner cruise on the *Marigalante*, an exact replica of the famous *Santa Maria* from Columbus's voyage to the new world. There's a reason those boat cruises are called "booze cruises." Booze, included in the price of the cruise, flowed freely—margaritas, piña coladas and beer, followed by tequila shots. We are lightweight drinkers, and it didn't take much to make us silly and to cause me some confusion. My daughter laughed at me as I watched the moon, wondering why it kept moving higher then lower. No one told me the boat was rocking!

Luckily, the word "no" is the same in Spanish as it is in English, and we remembered to say "No!" to stop the free flow of booze. We left the boat still able to make our way back to the Malecon, the walkway along the ocean. Finding a bench to prop us up, we sat in the moonlight and watched the vacationers and locals as they partied and enjoyed the nightlife.

Those two trips were the first times I had traveled with my

children when we were all adults, vacationing as best friends, not as just mother and child. We're still best friends. And it won't be the last trip we enjoy together.

Steve and Susan in
Puerto Vallarta

Salvaging Mom's Sanity

by
Maureen Rogers

We were skeptical when our teenage son found his first car on the Internet at a bargain price. It was a newer model, a sporty little silver-blue compact with low miles. The seller claimed to be the original owner and proudly showed us the clean title.

Buyer beware. I should have heeded the voice inside my head. We soon discovered a suspicious dent in the trunk and missing air bags, and when the new title finally arrived in the mail, the word "SALVAGE" popped out in the description. Evidently, an insurance company had declared the car totaled and our seller had purchased and rebuilt it. Back then, it took several weeks for an out-of-state title to be processed and by the time it arrived, the buyer had skipped town. Without the history, we had no idea if the thing had rolled off a 50-foot cliff or had been sideswiped by a semi. How long it would survive was anyone's guess.

The good news was that our son finally had his own wheels—we were off the hook as the parental shuttle service. Then late one night, the phone rang and I leapt out of bed. Our son was calling from the restaurant where he worked, asking for a ride home. His car had been stolen from the mall parking lot.

I was almost relieved to hear the car was gone. Of course, like any decent stroke of bad luck, it wasn't over that easily. The police called a day or two later to say they'd found it. Our son called from the station when he picked it up. "They found it at another mall across town." He chuckled. "No big deal, Mom. I guess the thieves had more shopping to do. You know how bad the bus system is around here." The gas tank was empty and $2 in change was missing, but they'd removed all his trash. He was happy—his ride was still intact.

A few weeks later, I got another phone call. "Mom, I just had an accident." I knew for sure that wheeled monstrosity was cursed. In my mind's eye, I saw it rolling off that 50-foot cliff, taking my son with it.

He groaned at my reaction. "Geez, don't go psycho, Mom. It's just a fender-bender. The woman ran into the back of me at a stoplight." He laughed. "She said she sneezed and forgot to brake. Her insurance will cover the damage. It'll be good as new."

"Yeah, right," I said. "It was never good as new—that thing is cursed."

Months went by without incident and I began to think

maybe I'd been overreacting. Then one day a police officer knocked on our door, looking for our son. He was in college by then and lived near campus in the city. The police said they had found his vehicle smashed and abandoned in a rural area miles north of town.

I panicked, envisioning his body strewn in some murky ditch, unconscious, slashed and bleeding or lying half-dead in a hospital with no one to identify him. I grabbed the phone, fingers trembling, stabbing at the numbers. It rang twice . . . three times . . . Finally, he picked up and I literally screamed with joy.

"What do you mean, my car's wrecked?" I could hear the not-this-again tone in his voice. "Wait a minute." After a long pause, he returned to the phone. "I don't know what you're talking about—the car's right here, parked out front."

The police officer took the phone from my hand and asked my son to go outside and check his license plates. Sure enough, they'd been switched. His plates had ended up on the abandoned, stolen car found out north.

I was more than a little delighted when our son realized the car was a strain on his college budget and decided to sell it . . . until I found out his older brother was the buyer. "Don't be ridiculous, Mom. I need the money, he needs a commuter car. It's the perfect solution." Both boys laughed at my paranoia. To them, the idea of a curse was just some weird figment of their mother's overactive imagination.

Fortunately, my older son only drove it for a few months then traded it in at a local dealership for a brand new car. Hallelujah! Finally the bad-luck mobile was gone. Our family was rid of it before a serious accident occurred.

But again, it wasn't quite that easy. The dealership that had accepted the car as a trade-in all of a sudden decided they had made a mistake by overlooking the salvage condition written on the title. They actually threatened our older son with a lawsuit if he didn't pay more money or take the car back. After a few weeks of harassment, we read in the paper that the dealership had fallen into bankruptcy and soon after that, they were out of business. The curse had transferred. That sporty little silver-blue coupe was more of a hex than I even realized!

Months later, I spotted the salvaged beast in a downtown parking lot. I recognized the license plate numbers and froze. I thought about sticking around to warn the new owner, but decided against it. I didn't care if our boys thought their mother was crazy—our family had been curse-free for almost a year and I wasn't about to mess with fate.

Maureen's son and "the car"

In Tune with My Son

by
Terri Elders

As my birthday neared this past year, I wondered what my son would choose this time. What events would he recreate? Which of my life's milestones would he bring into sharp focus through the medium of music?

In 1964, when *I Wanna Hold Your Hand* hit American pop charts, Steve was only six, but he listened raptly when I chattered about my high school journalism students dancing the Frug and the Watusi on the *Lloyd Thaxton Show*, airing from nearby Los Angeles.

Because his dad worked nights, Steve and I had evenings to ourselves. While I corrected homework papers, we listened on the radio to legendary sportscaster Vin Scully call the play-by-play for our beloved Dodgers. Or, we strolled to the library to stock up on his favorite Dr. Seuss and Maurice Sendak storybooks.

Now we began to follow rock and roll. We tuned in the dance shows of the day, *Shindig, Hullabaloo*, Dick Clark's

American Bandstand. Steve spent his allowance joining Beatles fan clubs. I heard empathy in his voice as he read to me from the newsletters about children in Kenya and the Philippines that the clubs sponsored for tuition and books.

Sometimes we brought our BLTs and lemonade into the living room, dining while we caught up on the latest scoop. "Listen to what George Harrison's sister says!" Steve would exclaim, excited at having a personal connection with one of the Fab Four.

In the meantime, my high school students also transitioned from the Beach Boys and Jan and Dean to the British Invasion. "Which side would you take?" I asked Steve, discussing debates on the merits of The Dave Clark Five versus Herman's Hermits. Steve remained loyal to the mop-top Beatles, his "fave raves." We lamented not securing tickets to the Hollywood Bowl appearances, and, in 1966, envied our neighbor who took her sons to the concert at Dodger Stadium.

By 1968, Steve hunkered down at the kitchen counter every Wednesday night as KHJ's Sam Riddle counted down the *Boss 30* radio show in Los Angeles. He meticulously recorded the hits one by one in his blue notebook. He already had been collecting singles for well over a year. In the meantime, I had changed jobs, so I now raced down Interstate 405 toward the Cudahy Department of Public Social Services office, and encouraged by Steve, also tuned to KHJ, grooving on the Beatles, the Box Tops, Linda Ronstadt and even all seven minutes and 11 seconds of Richard Harris' *MacArthur Park*.

"I hear music in my head," Steve once confided. I asked if he wanted to take piano or guitar lessons. "No," he confessed, "I just love to listen." Over the years, his collection stockpiled.

He turned from singles to LPs, and then to 8-tracks, cassettes and finally to CDs. In recent decades, he has shared some obscure cuts with Southland Golden Oldies radio stations.

When I joined the Peace Corps in 1987, Steve provided me with the first of his special gifts. He transferred to cassette all of the Beatles numbers from his albums. On balmy Saturday mornings in Belize City, the largest city in the Central American nation of Belize, I hand-laundered my towels and sheets while listening to *Your Mother Should Know* and *Magical Mystery Tour.*

The first time capsule arrived a few years ago on my birthday. Steve had gone through his collection and made me a tape of the top songs from fall 1967 to spring 1968, which was my first year with the Department of Public Social Services. Now retired and living in the country in northwest Washington state, I played the tapes every time I made the 70-mile drive to Spokane. As I listened to The Cowsills, Lulu and other chart toppers of that era, I felt the years rolling back. Once again I become 30 years old, driving around Los Angeles, waiting for my future to unfold with each song, each mile, each day.

At Christmas, another tape arrived. This time Steve chose my 21st birthday, which occurred just a few months after he had been born. Until I played my gift tape, I had forgotten carrying infant Steve around the house, boogying to Bobby Darin's *Splish Splash* and two-stepping to Laurie London's *He's Got the Whole World in His Hands.*

When I opened my package on my 70th birthday, memories of 1955, the year Steve's dad and I married, flooded back. Steve had labeled the tape, "Terri's 18th Birthday—Plus," and had recorded what he said was, and I quote, "a nice mix of the old music fighting for time with the new rock 'n' roll," along with highlights from that summer and fall.

And sure enough, there it all was, the songs that his dad and I courted to, Roger Williams' romantic ballad, *Autumn Leaves*, following Chuck Berry's *Maybelline*. As if it were only yesterday, I remember getting seasick on the Catalina ferry as we sailed back from our Avalon honeymoon, decorating our first apartment with the wedding gifts, snagging my first full-time job at Pacific Tel and Tel.

The tapes continue to arrive each June and each December, providing me with background music for my life's review. Marcel Proust's hero in *Remembrance of Things Past* had memories triggered by the taste of a madeleine cookie. Other people claim to remember best through scents. For me, though, nothing tugs the elusive shadows of my past into the shimmering sunlight of this current moment like the songs on my time capsules.

Steve's tapes are candid snapshots of my life, framed in melody.

Terri and Steve

Baby Doll
on Campus

by
Rose Ella Putnam

My husband and I decided to drive from Klamath Falls, Oregon over to the Southern Oregon College campus in Ashland to celebrate our daughter's birthday. It was her first birthday away from home and we were all a little lonesome for her.

We planned to take our daughter and her girlfriends out to dinner to celebrate, but we hadn't expected quite so many friends! We took them to a nice, trendy restaurant at the edge of the campus grounds where we were thankful to learn that they did not sell alcohol. As parents, we continued to worry about our children even after they left home, so we hoped our daughter chose this alcohol-free place when she went out.

The girls had the next week off. When it was time for us to go home, the girls who lived in Klamath Falls pleaded with me to spend the night in the dorm and drive them home the next day. Our sons had driven over in a separate car, so it was no problem to have her daddy ride back home with them.

Because I had not planned to spend the night, I had not packed any nightclothes, makeup or extra clothes. The girls quickly said, "No problem," as they could borrow a nightie for me from one of their—shall we say—heftier friends. I was considerably larger than my daughter and her roommate were and I could not wear their nighties.

After dragging in a cot for me, I prepared for bed. I washed out all of my unmentionables and found, to my dismay, that the short, ruffled baby doll nightie they had borrowed didn't come with panties.

With little ceremony, I donned the ruffles and quickly got into bed. After listening to what seemed like endless conversation and giggles from the girls, I finally fell asleep.

In the middle of the night, the fire bell rang. The girls hopped up and one of them said, "We've got to get out of here!" As they grabbed their robes, I informed them that I wasn't going anywhere dressed like that, in high heels, baby doll pajamas—minus the panties—and no coat. I would just stay in the room, I told them.

My daughter threw a robe at me and said, "You have to get out or we'll get in trouble!" Her robe would have fit just one of my arms and one side, but I wrapped it around my waist to get as much coverage as possible. All the girls from the dorm laughed hysterically when I emerged from the room.

As we were just ready to step out the dorm door into the night, one of the larger students saw my plight and threw me her coat. She was wearing pajamas and didn't need it. There on the hill beside the college dorm stood all of the boys from the dorm across the way. They stood watching the commotion and I hope all the whistles and catcalls were for the girls, not for me.

Once officials announced that it had been a false alarm, students were free to return to the dorms. When we got back into the room, all I could hear while I tried to sleep were giggles and guffaws coming from rooms up and down the hall.

As I fell asleep, I thought to myself, *Was that what I got for being a good parent and staying over to drive the girls? Why so much laughter? Hadn't they ever seen a mama in high heels wearing a ruffled baby doll?*

Landing an Invitation

by
John J. Lesjack

We sat close together, bouncing along in the tow truck. Our eyes absorbed dashboard knobs, dials and levers. The CB radio noises amused us. We laughed at the cars below us in the freeway traffic. We enjoyed riding high.

"This is neat, Dad!" My son's six-year-old voice radiated joy and I hugged him. How often does a father enjoy a ride in the vehicle of his son's dreams? Often enough? Never mind that my car had broken down.

At age nine, impatient for school to end and summer vacation to begin, he asked, "Dad, can we go camping soon?"

We pitched our tent on a bluff overlooking a little lake in a beautiful valley. During the day, we fished for largemouth bass, which, when caught, we then released. At night, we kept the tent flap open and looked at the sky.

"Oh, neat!" my son exclaimed with each shooting star. We

made our private wishes.

The night sky entertained him until he fell asleep, secure in his sleeping bag beside mine. Our good time together under the stars went all too quickly.

At age 16, he reminded me, "I didn't ask to live here."

"You keep that attitude and you won't be," I informed him. *Who is this teenager who came to live with me? Why are we adversaries,* I wondered. *Does the divorce still trouble him? Is someone at school picking on him?*

He didn't say.

Regardless, he's mine and he's precious to me, but he did make me wonder how someone who was once so close could have become so emotionally distant.

The prodigal son stage lasted only until he graduated from high school, even though it seemed like it lasted forever. Then he went to junior college.

"Dad, you always said we should be careful what we ask for, because we may get it." My son sat on the couch with his girlfriend, who was also a junior college student. He had my attention. He had trained me to be patient with him and to keep my heart and mind open.

"You've been asking for a grandchild," he said. "I am here to tell you that we are going to make you a grandpa. What do you think of that?"

My heart went *ka-thump.*

Stunned, ecstatic, surprised, *very surprised,* fighting back tears and trying to keep from dancing a jig, I stayed calm and handed out congratulations.

The young couple traveled to Ohio to visit her parents.

My son called late one night. "I proposed and she accepted!" He nearly shouted into the telephone. "Dad, I want you to be the first one to know that when we get back to California, we will be getting married!"

I had complained that I was always the last one to know what was going on in my son's life. He took that to heart. He shared this major moment with *me* first. He still has no idea how precious he is to me.

My son and his fiancé married on the beach and had a small reception.

Fatherhood began for my son with the cutting of the cord in the delivery room. He immediately bonded with his daughter. A gentleness and deep compassion surrounded him in his fatherly duties. Using a voice more mellow than any he ever heard from me, he cleaned, fed and nurtured his daughter. I marveled at my son's parenting skills and held him in awe. After all, he was only 21.

He balanced family life with his college work and first earned a bachelor's degree at 23 and a year later, a master of science degree. Such achievements are unheard of in our family tree.

Despite his full schedule and long hours, he took time while away at college to send a letter to me that ended with, "I hope to fish for largemouth bass with you soon. Maybe we'll land one this time."

I like my son.

Our next visit was too brief. Soon, standing on my front porch, we were again saying goodbye. They were moving out of the country for jobs. "And I won't see you for three years. Right?"

"Not unless you come to Germany," my son said.

"Your wife is four months pregnant," I reminded him.

"Dad," he said, as if he were the adult, "babies are born in Germany all the time."

I tried again to reel him in. "Well, are you coming back to California?"

He took a deep breath, and then said in the mellow voice he uses on his daughter, "We haven't planned that far ahead."

Long pause. I hadn't set the hook.

When he was a little boy, my son and I held hands when we walked together. Back then, I could pick him up and hug him. By the end of fifth grade, he had stopped handholding with me, but a hug had become traditional.

I reached up and hugged him. "I love you, son." He hugged me back, picked me up and set me down.

"I love you, Dad."

"I'll miss you, son."

"I'll miss you, Dad."

He drove off and left me with my thoughts. *Why hadn't I told him he had turned out all right and that I am proud of him? With a few more words, he would have known I love who he is as a person, not what he does, like his volunteer work in kinder-garten class. Just him. Unconditionally.* I didn't say that because all I could think of was that he had been home a year and not once had we fished for largemouth bass!

His postcard arrived and I sat on the porch with it a long time and I thought about my son's adventurous life. He rock climbs, the card said, visits towns with names I can't pronounce, and studies German. Whoever he is now, he's doing a good job of living his life.

In my son's house, he is thought of as a husband and father, and soon another person will arrive and call him "Daddy." He's a package deal, now. He belongs to all of us, technically, but more so to the family he's created. The distance between father and son is increasing, naturally and respectfully.

We'll get close to each other again, but we'll never really close the entire distance between us. He's over there in his world—Germany—a place I've never been. Future times together will be by invitation. We won't live together under the same roof anymore, maybe not even in the same town or state or country. And that's OK. We've ridden the tow truck together, made our wishes on shooting stars and fished together.

With passport in hand, I'll soon visit my son and his family in Germany. I landed an invitation. Catch and release is our style.

Damon
and John

The Other Side of the Coin

Parents do the darndest things!

A Kodak Moment

by
Cappy Hall Rearick

It was the best of times, it was the worst of times. It was Valentine's Day *and* it was my birthday.

I have a photo of the party that my parents threw for me the year I turned six years old. It is a day that will live in my personal infamy. Daddy took the photo with a Kodak camera Mama made him buy especially for the occasion. The photograph shows 10 small bodies seated in a circle on Mama's living room floor.

For my birthday, Mama made me a red velvet jumper and a white ruffled blouse. I wore shiny black patent leather Mary Jane shoes and plain white socks on my little feet that were stuck straight out in front of me in the photo. Daddy was no Ansel Adams, so he simply snapped the photo, feet and all. My Mary Janes look big enough in that photo to fit a kangaroo.

In the photo, we balanced limp paper plates on our laps and shoveled strawberry ice cream and Mama's homemade red velvet cake into our mouths. Only one kid out of the bunch was still wearing front teeth. Only one.

The dining room table in the background of the picture was draped with Mama's good white tablecloth. Because it was also Valentine's Day, Mama had constructed red hearts, fastening them together with paste that tasted like spearmint. She then scattered and straight-pinned them all over the tablecloth. There was crepe paper, red of course, stretched and curled and Scotch-taped to the chandelier, and from the looks of it, anything else she could reach.

We giggled and smiled when Daddy took the first photo, and then we grinned again for the next one. It was only after Daddy said, "OK, kids. One more time,'" that all hell broke loose. Daddy had an obsessive streak that sneaked out every time he got hold of a new gadget, and the Kodak was his flavor of the week. He should have stopped while he was ahead.

Stewart Hill, the youngest of the party guests, was known for his weak stomach. "I don't feel good," he said while Daddy fiddled with the Kodak.

"Just a minute, Stewart," Daddy muttered. "We're almost done. Only one more."

"Yes sir, but I *really* don't feel good." Stewart was turning greener with every click of the Kodak.

Stewart was known as a rough and tumble kid, no stranger to neighborhood brawls. He had to defend himself because he was constantly being teased about his heavy glasses that were almost always down toward the end of his nose and cocked over to one side. His glasses, sitting all cockeyed like that, often made his stomach queasy. Red velvet cake and ice cream didn't help. Daddy should have realized that, but he was too enamored with his new toy.

Stewart moaned once and threw up.

The paper plate of red velvet cake he was holding flew up in the air and landed on top of Ann McGee's head. What came out of Stewart's mouth headed, like a guided missile, straight for my black patent leather Mary Janes.

In less than a nanosecond, Stewart Hill transformed my birthday party into *Hell's Kitchen*.

Ann was screaming; Stewart was heaving. Will Walkup was jumping up and down, pointing at Stewart, whose face had now turned Key-lime green. Billy Glover was last seen running, head down, toward the front door and Mary Sims, the epitome of ladylikeness even at age six, pointedly averted her eyes to it all.

I stared at my feet and tried not to lose what I had eaten of the heart-shaped red velvet birthday cake, while the rest of the crowd took turns jumping around the room like peeper frogs after a summer rain.

Mama tripped over the coffee table trying to get to Stewart before he threw up again. She said a string of cuss words that six-year-old children love to repeat, while Daddy simply stood in the middle of the chaos holding the Kodak like it was the Holy Grail.

Finally, he snapped out of his stupor long enough to play Pied Piper and lead the hysterical kids outside for some much needed fresh air and a wild game of pin the tail on the donkey. In our case, the game was retitled to "pin the heart on the cupid," since Mama was going through one of her adult creative phases.

When the party was over, nobody opted to take home leftover birthday cake like kids always did. Even now, I can't look at a piece of red velvet cake.

The very next day, Mama had to have the living room rug dry cleaned due to the 10 plates of ice cream and cake stomped into the wool by 10 sets of tiny feet.

Daddy never got the hang of taking pictures, but eventually my brother fished the dusty Kodak out of the closet. He developed the long forgotten snapshots Daddy had taken at my sixth birthday party—or, as it has become known in our family over the years since—the St. Valentine's Day Massacre.

Stewart (far left) and Cappy (third from the left)

Miss America or Misadventure

by
Janet Sheppard Kelleher

My mother wanted me to be Miss America. I know this because she made me watch the annual pageant with her on television. I know this because she gave me a Shirley Temple perm when I was five years old. I know this because she made me take tap and ballet at the fine Roy McCollough School of Dance. And I hated it. All of it—crinolines, tapping-shoe sounds, makeup, hair bows—and I especially hated tights and tutus!

By age eight, I'd perfected the art of persuasion by listening to my brothers con my parents. Mom gave my hair back to me—no more Shirley Temple perm—and allowed me to quit dance if I would agree to work in my grandmother's grocery store on Saturdays. It was a fair trade. I'd have done anything to eradicate costumes and lipstick.

My mother's expectations for me seemed far-fetched. First, the outdoors had me from *day one*. I loved playing kickball with the neighborhood kids. I fished with Daddy whenever he would put up with someone who wasn't endowed with a pointer and couldn't wee-wee off the side of a boat.

I rode my bike with cardboard held in place against the spokes with clothespins, which made a fun clicking sound when I rode, eagerly awaiting the day a real car motor would putt-putt into my life. When I played outside, I didn't go in until one of my parents honked the car horn three short beeps, signaling nighttime was upon us and I should get my little carcass home.

Other girls learned to play tennis in their cute little skirts. I learned to bowl like the devil, just to impress my famous older brother Jimmie, the state bowling champ.

While friends took piano and voice lessons, I studied karate. It seemed ultimately more practical. When needed, I could beat the pulp out of somebody—I mean lay 'em flat—instead of hollering like an opera singer, hoping to sing them half to death.

The real deciding factor occurred, however, when Briggs & Stratton built the minibike. This 15-year-old curled up into her loving daddy's lap and begged him for motorized wheels. Somehow, he convinced Mom I'd be careful. I was. But accidents happen. And when my foot got caught up under the foot pedal, it bent completely backward and practically ripped off. The injury was so bad that my foot had to be screwed back on. I could never again walk well in heels—my ankle wouldn't quite bend far enough.

And with that ankle injury came the crowning blow. Poor

Mom. She had wanted Bert Parks to sing for me: "There she is, Miss America."

The sad fact is that the only thing I had going for me was my hair. I created a flip that could make Mary Tyler Moore jealous. Then college came with my hippie phase, and my one claim to beauty evaporated like grain alcohol at a fraternity party. I gave up the perfect coiffure for practical wash-and-wear styles. These styles served me well and saved my babies from hearing some choice words when they upchucked in my hair—words my father made famous whenever I'd cast my fishing lure into an oak tree or a brush pile.

I dashed Mom's dreams. She wanted me to be a beautiful, culturally talented lady. I wanted to dissect frogs, solve math equations and break bricks with my hand. You can't perform ballet in bowling shoes. Or show off your new karate gi in the evening gown competition.

I hated to disappoint my mother. We all do. But can't you just see me limping down the beauty pageant runway in draw-string-waist Karate pants, showing off one high heel and one bare foot, the latter with a prominent ankle scar resembling football laces? Can't you picture the shiny yellow bowling shirt sporting my name on the pocket and a 250 Club patch on the sleeve? And Bert Parks singing, "There she goes, Miss Twinkle Toes." Mom, in the audience, would be asking herself, *Where, oh where, did I go wrong?*

So Mom didn't get Miss America for her daughter. She got instead a spirited, independent woman who lives to learn, a woman who emotes like nobody's watching, sucking the marrow out of life and daring anyone to find fault with that. I wonder if Mom was happy getting Misadventure for a daughter instead of Miss America. When I glide my Jazzy Scooter ever so gracefully onto that big runway in the sky, totally spent from my misadventures, I'll be sure to ask her.

Janet, then and now

Just Call Me Gypsy

by
Kathleene S. Baker

My parents would probably say I was a pretty decent teenager. However, I created my fair share of havoc and participated in plenty of foolhardy rowdiness. It's just a darned good thing I wasn't caught. After bringing up two hell-raising boys, I guess Mom and Dad expected their only daughter would naturally behave like a lady at all times. Well, where's the fun in that? And is it really something one comes by naturally? I don't think so—I know so.

At some point in time, my parents obviously took classes at the no-nonsense school of parenting, with Dad making straight A's. The reason I say this is because I could persuade Mom to bend the rules or at least consider new ideas. Being a woman, she seemed to understand teenage girls and their whims. However, Dad had definite ideas and would not budge, come hell or high water. We weren't Catholic, but I often felt he was raising me to become a nun.

Dad was as rigid as a stone statue when it came to his opinions. Being stylish meant nothing to him—it was his way or the highway! Two fussing teenage daughters might have softened him up, but I had no sister to join ranks with me. Alas, I was on my own.

Our first major conflict arose when I asked to have my ears pierced. Mother seemed open to the idea, but said I'd need to run it by Dad. Anything that required Dad's OK made me anxious, but after dinner that very evening, I broached the subject with him.

"Dad, would it be OK if I got my ears pierced? Everyone is having it done and my birthday is coming up. It would be the perfect gift." My voice sounded angelic.

He looked at me like I'd told him the moon was square. I waited for a reply, but none came.

"So, what do you think?" I prodded.

"I think we'll talk about it when you're a little older," he mumbled.

The tone of his mumble said it all. I bristled.

"Older? I'm going to be 16! How much older do I need to be? I don't think you will ever let me have my ears pierced—will you?"

I still remember his words as if it were yesterday, "No, you will not have your ears pierced! No daughter of mine is going to run around looking like a damned gypsy!" His translucent blue eyes shot daggers at me.

All my willpower was required not to reply, "Doesn't bother me if I look like one!"

With no chance of winning the battle, I marched to my

bedroom and pouted. Should I have spouted off one more time, I'd likely never have married; I'd still be grounded and living at home with him. I'm serious! Talking back to my parents was not tolerated and could command a death sentence.

I knew nothing about gypsies, although I had seen them in a few movies. Mindful of their long, dark hair, colorful clothes, flowing scarves and scads of bobbles and bangles, I thought they looked pretty snazzy. Still, traveling about the country in a gaudy, rickety wagon left me completely puzzled. They surely froze during winter months, only to smother during summer heat beneath all of those long flowing garments. At least they had enough sense to go barefoot during hot weather.

Shortly after leaving home and going out on my own, I had my ears pierced. It was at the top of my priority list. I scrimped and saved for several months in order to afford the procedure. My parents came to visit soon after that. Excited about my piercings, but not wanting to cause too much trouble, I wore small stud earrings. I'm positive that's not at all what Dad had expected—I bet he envisioned long, dangly bangles that rested on both of my shoulders.

"Well, Dad, I did it. Do I look like a gypsy?" I teased while pulling my long hair back to give him a good view.

"Not exactly—and at least they aren't huge," he answered. He seemed relieved.

I didn't realize it at the time, but that one single act of piercing my ears and proving my point opened the gateway for generations to come.

Dad didn't even pitch a fit about my first niece and his first granddaughter having pierced ears, and at a much younger age than I had been. Two more granddaughters followed suit several years later. Then, miracle of all miracles, Mom debuted with holes in her ears. Stunned doesn't even describe my reaction. For years she had endured clip earrings that pinched like the devil and one always fell off when she spoke on the phone. I was darn proud of her for getting her ears pierced. But the biggest surprise was yet to come—Dad gave Mom diamond studs for Christmas one year!

Then, when I least expected it, I was smacked right in the face with déjà vu! My husband nearly had a conniption fit when our daughter wanted a second ear piercing. It had become a "must" during Leisa's high school years. Truthfully, I kind of liked the look myself, a small stud in the top hole and a larger earring below. I didn't intervene, assuming in due time he would come around. And if not, I would plead Leisa's case. He was being plain ridiculous over the whole thing.

A few weeks later, Leisa and I found ourselves at the mall with a shopping list. We strolled from shop to shop, and there, right before our eyes, appeared a piercing kiosk. Leisa didn't ask or even pause; her dad had already laid down the law. On the other hand, my feet froze right where I stood. *By golly,* I reasoned, *I like the look, I am a grown woman and getting your ears pierced isn't against the law.* I made my decision within seconds.

Several days passed before my husband noticed that Leisa and I both had a couple of new holes in our heads. And I told Leisa I would gladly take the heat.

Amazingly, he admitted the look wasn't bad at all.

I couldn't keep my mouth shut. "So, what did you think we were going to do, wear lug bolts in the top holes?"

Leisa exploded with laughter, I began to giggle and eventually my husband even chuckled. All was well with the world once again!

Over the course of many years, every female in the family was running amok with pierced ears. And eventually Dad's only grandson went through a wacky phase, which resulted in him wearing a stud in one ear. Dad did shake his head at that news, but it was soon forgotten when said grandson became a firefighter. And finally, when a great granddaughter came along, she naturally joined ranks with the rest of us pierced beauties.

Long story short and many years later, in the end Dad became the proud patriarch of a band of outrageous gypsies!

Kathleene the Gypsy

Lukewarm Milk

by
Kendall Roderick

I didn't know what a "parent" was growing up. It wasn't until I got older that I understood that parents are just children, who by having children became parents. Easy enough? What I hadn't noticed was that by using this particular formula, a child had actually raised me.

I was the first-born, the one who taught the child to be a parent. I'd like to take credit but it was involuntary.

My parent-in-training was good at what she did. She took care of me. Every day she picked me up from school and always parked in the same spot. I saw her car immediately. But to get to the car, I had to go down three sets of concrete stairs and around all the school buses that lined up daily on the street. Every day, I passed the idling buses, and their exhaust fumes from the rear of each vehicle hit me at nearly eye level. Those fumes always sat heavy in my lungs, and the sickening smell stayed with me all the way to my mom's car.

I knew what would be waiting for me when I got to the car—a snack and a plastic cup of milk that had warmed while she waited for me. As I approached, I could see the silhouette of my mother's head inside the car. Snow and mud clung to my boots. Looking both ways before crossing the street, I made it to our car and opened its heavy passenger door. I hated sitting in the back of the car and longed for the day I'd sit in the front seat, like a grown-up.

"Hi, honey. How was your day?" She always started the engine right away and looked behind her seat to hand me the plastic cup. The milk sloshed back and forth and my stomach turned. I hoped this time the milk wouldn't be lukewarm. We only lived three minutes away, so I'm sure I could have waited for my snack. "Here are your cookies." I grabbed the folded paper towel and unwrapped the morsels. If I hurried and put them into my mouth, maybe I could avoid talking.

"Honey," she said, her voice slightly spiked, "how was your day?"

The cookie completely filled every corner of my mouth, but still I pushed out the words. "I got in trouble today."

"You did?" The reverse motion of the car came to a sudden halt and the milk threatened to jump over the cup's edge. "What happened?"

Key to being a parent: ask questions first.

"I hit Joey Johnson in the head with a stick." It sounded worse than it had been. Really, I had been playing fetch with a dog when Joey got in the way.

"You did what?" If all fails, ask more questions—maybe

the answer will change.

"I hit Joey Johnson in the head with a stick." My answer didn't change.

"The boy with the man-head?"

"I don't know."

"Really bushy eyebrows?"

"Yeah."

"Why did you hit him in the head?"

"It was an accident. I was playing fetch."

"With the boy who has a man's head?" she asked.

"He doesn't have a man's head, Mom."

"He does. His head is abnormally large for his body."

Note: Parents come up with weird memory triggers to remember their child's classmates.

"I wasn't playing with him; there was a dog."

"So you got confused?"

"Mom!"

"Well, honey, I just don't see how you could have hit him when you were playing fetch with a dog."

Known fact: parents don't understand.

"So?" she asked, waiting for my response.

"What, Mom?" My tone became irritated and whiny. I didn't want to tell her.

"Is he hurt?" I awkwardly pushed another cookie into my mouth. "Kendall!"

"One second." I slowly chewed and swallowed, sipping down the lukewarm milk. I heard the impatience in her tapping fingers as they hit the steering wheel. I hadn't done anything wrong before. It was a first for both of us. "His head started bleeding."

"Kendall!"

When parents don't know what to say, they repeat your name like it's a curse word. As a kid, repeat what parent does. "Mom!"

"Did you go to the principal's office?" she asked. Obviously, when the name-calling doesn't work, ask more questions.

"Uh-huh."

Within a split second, she parked the car again, a parental multitasking that is equivalent to magic. "How badly?"

"Not badly."

"Hospital?"

"No."

"Will I get a call from his mother?" I hoped not. Parents calling parents about their children is worse than a hospital visit. "Do I need to call his mom?"

"No, no! Mom, please don't do that!"

Being a parent takes some special handling of a child. Those days, boys were unpredictable. Years later, when I was in my teens, my mother and I went to the grocery store. A boy approached and addressed me by name. I didn't recognize him, but he told me we went to elementary school together and when I asked how he remembered me, he said, "How can I forget the girl who threw a stick at my head?" It was Joey, all grown up. My face flushed as I said my goodbyes and went back to my mother, who stood only a few feet away in line.

That's when I noticed the jug of milk in the cart. I suspected it would be lukewarm by the time we got home. "Well, he is handsome," Mom said. "I'm sure glad he grew into his man-head."

"Mother!"

The Trip

by
Ellen Denton

A mom's sixth sense about what's going on with her children is probably natural to mothers everywhere, but it hit light speed with my own mother during one incident that occurred years ago.

My mother had never flown in an airplane. The very idea of doing so gave her heart palpitations. I had no such fears, but my being on a plane terrified her as much as the idea of her being on one. She worried about the plane crashing, being hijacked or tilting in turbulence, causing a cup of blistering-hot coffee to splash into my face. She envisioned suitcases flying out of luggage racks and careening off cabin walls. And she worried about collisions with passing meteorites. She even once brought up the subject of UFO abductions!

When I was in my 30s, I lived in California, and she, in New York. I would occasionally have to fly for work-related reasons. To spare her the upset this would cause, I did my best to make sure she didn't find out about it. It wasn't very hard to cover up that I'd taken a short trip to another city or state, but one day, there was an upcoming flight that I would not be able to hide.

I was going to fly to England and would probably be there for about two months. It was one thing to juggle the timing on a few phone calls and, with the help of my husband, hide that I was in some other American city, but another thing entirely to conceal the fact that I'd left the country for two months. I won't even go into Mom's many phobias regarding other countries and all the mysterious, exotic diseases she conceived to be ever present in any place other than America, regardless of how civilized and modern that country might be.

I pondered how to break the news to her. I knew she would envision me bobbing around in the ocean in a bright yellow life jacket after the inevitable plane crash. If I lived through that, she would then agonize over my being in another country, what with all the shady foreigners shuffling evilly by me, not to mention the many unhygienic, disease-ridden public toilets.

Finally, I figured out the best way to tell her. Mothers love to hear about the good things that happen to their children. Nothing ever made my mother happier than learning about some success or honor I had achieved. I had in the past, both when I was still living in New York and later in California, called her and started a conversation with, "Something really great happened," or "I have good news!"

She would eagerly and immediately ask me about it with a "TELL ME! TELL ME! TELL ME!" Then she'd press me for all the details.

That's how I decided to approach the subject of my upcoming trip. I would present it as a great career opportunity and a great honor that I was selected to do this project, with a lot of *yada, yada, yada* added in here and there. That way, I could focus her attention on all the good aspects of it, instead of on the fears and worries.

When the time came, I called her, starting the conversation with, "Mom, I have the most wonderful news!"

Then I waited for the, "TELL ME! TELL ME! TELL ME!" It never came. After a few moments of dead silence on her end of the line, she shrieked, "OH, GOD NO! YOU'RE GOING TO EUROPE! PLEASE! JUST DON'T TELL ME YOU'RE GOING TO EUROPE!"

There was not one, single, solitary reason why she should have even *suspected* I might be going to Europe, or anywhere else overseas. It truly was a mother's sixth sense.

We both had a good laugh about this later—*much* later—and long after I was safely back from England.

Musically Gifted

by
Carole Fowkes

Being a child of the Sixties, I loved its music, from the soulful sounds of Motown to the otherworldly sounds of long-haired boys in skin-tight bellbottom pants and flowered shirts. I identified with it all.

As much as this music seemed a part of my youth, though, my family's finances were such that I could only listen to this music from my radio, a portable blue transistor model handed down from my older sister, Vicki. So I contented myself with hearing the latest albums with my friends. While the times I listened to music playing on their turntables, or record players as they called them, were great fun, it made me long for my own small suitcase-like record player and albums which I could listen to in teenage moody solitude.

My parents struggled to raise two children on my father's limited pay as a factory worker. Although they supplied my sister and me with decent clothes and an occasional dinner out at the nearby inexpensive family restaurant, no extra money existed for luxuries such as a record player. And no amount of pleading, cajoling or moping about could convince them that a record player was a necessity to a teenager, without which she would surely perish from unpopularity. They told me I'd have to wait until I was old enough to get a job to purchase one. But that was two years away, a lifetime to a young girl.

After Thanksgiving when I was 14, my mother began her usual tradition of asking Vicki and me to make our wish list for Christmas. Before I could even open my mouth with my usual request for a turntable, she warned me in a stern voice, "No stereo. You know we can't afford it, so no use asking."

I sighed dramatically, rolled my eyes, and, as if they had asked me to scrub the floor on my hands and knees, I listed shoes, mittens and clothes, all the usual stuff, expecting to be unsurprised with my presents. Still, I looked forward, as I did every year, to opening gifts and watching my parents' look of excitement as my sister and I cooed over the latest new sweater or skirt.

As Christmas approached, with my sister as instigator, Vicki and I hunted for packages my mother took the time to hide. She changed the place each year, but we never failed to find every beautifully wrapped gift. We'd shake the box, feel its weight and guess what it held. This year, though, my sister teased me. "Have you noticed there are more presents for me than you? I guess Mom and Dad finally realized I deserve to be their favorite."

"That's not true," I retorted with bravado. "Mom just bought yours first, you know, saving the best for last." But in secret, I thought maybe she ran out of money and couldn't buy anything else for me. I started to look for clues that we had less money than usual. One day I even asked my sister, "Have you noticed all the pasta we've been having for the past few weeks? No meat?"

She rolled her eyes. As my older sister, she often acted as if I had been some village's idiot my parents rescued.

Finally Christmas morning came and my father tiptoed into our room early, as he'd done every year for as long as I could remember. Then, as he also did each year, in a booming voice he announced it was time for us to get up and open presents. Vicki and I, trying to pretend we were too grown up to be excited, dragged ourselves out of bed, yawning and stretching as we put on our robes.

I sauntered out of the bedroom first and realized my sister's observation had been right. There were more presents for her than me. I heard Nat King Cole singing *The Christmas Song,* but ignored the familiar tune, trying to reconcile my lesser share of presents. I concluded they had run out of money. Feeling very mature, I decided to make the best of it for my parents' sake.

But my father watched me with a smile on his face. "That sounds pretty good, doesn't it?" he asked me.

At first, I wasn't sure what he meant. I realized then he meant the music. I shrugged, uninterested in listening to a song I'd been hearing everywhere for the past four weeks. Before I sat down by the tree, he asked me to get him some more coffee. I thought his request was strange, since his cup was far from empty. But I trudged toward the kitchen, where the music grew louder. No radio on, though. Forgetting the coffee, I started down the stairs, into the basement recreation room. My father crept up behind me, followed by my mother and Vicki.

When I reached the bottom of the stairs, I looked into the room and saw the source of the music: a big Magnavox stereo console with a small turntable in the center and huge speakers covered with brown mesh fabric interwoven with golden threads.

"Do you like it?" My parents asked, almost in unison.

I looked at the gift and for a brief second, I thought to protest, *No, I only wanted a small record player I could carry around. Not this. Not a piece of furniture.* But then I looked at their faces, my mother standing next to the stereo, a smile as generous as I knew her to be, and my father's face aglow with joy and pride to be giving me what I had wanted so much. Catching their happiness, I smiled as broadly as possible and hugged them both, thanking them over and over.

That day, I think I stepped a little closer to being an adult, understanding this wasn't just a gift of music for which they'd no doubt scrimped and saved—they had given me a gift of love. Realizing that, the music coming from the stereo sounded that much sweeter.

The Flagpole

by
Jerry Baker

"If you're not afraid—if you want to fight—just raise your hand."

Those words made my blood run cold, spoken by a bully named Bobby. I had been wondering when they would be meant for me, because every 11-year-old boy in my school had heard those same words. My time had finally come.

It was the 1950s. I lived in a less than prosperous neighborhood in Austin, Texas. In short, times were "by-God tough." The above-mentioned bully was a good 6 to 8 inches taller than the rest of us fifth graders, and he made everyone's life miserable.

Lunchtime was when he really threw his weight around. There wasn't much supervision in the schools back then and even less during our lunch period. No adults were there to ask if you, as a child, had any "issues." You were on your own, in every sense of the word.

"Well, since you won't raise your hand, I'll just teach you a lesson after school anyway," Bobby taunted.

And so, that afternoon, yours truly was yelled at, shoved and hit. To sum it up, I got whipped, ego and all. I don't recall the exact moment, but obviously I had told Mom about the fight when I got home from school, and she must have told Dad. How else would he have known?

After supper, I was on the floor of the living room listening to the radio. Dad was in his chair reading the newspaper. The open paper completely blocked the view of his face—I could only see his fingers grasping the pages on each side.

Dad was a man of very few words, so when he suddenly spoke, I'm jumped a little.

"Your mother told me about a little problem you had today."

"Yes sir," I answered.

"So, why don't you turn the radio down and tell me about it."

It wasn't pleasant, but I repeated the story of my miserable afternoon.

"And how do you feel about it?" Dad asked in his deep voice.

I told him how the aroma of food from the lunchroom smelled good, but, at the same time, made me sick, because I knew Bobby was coming to find me after school. It felt much like when you're starting to get the flu.

"That's fear, son, and fear must be managed. Now, the next time he asks you to raise your hand, it had better look like a goddamned flagpole!"

So I had two choices. I could remain a wimp, avoiding Bobby's challenges, or I could follow Dad's stern advice. Having been a Marine, Dad offered advice only once—and he expected you to act upon it. What I had to do was certain.

Over the next couple of weeks, I moved from getting whipped to becoming a formidable foe, able to hurt Bobby, at which time he disappeared. And guess what? When I was hit, it really didn't hurt. In summary, the entire process unfolded efficiently and quickly, and then was over.

The lesson, however, has always stayed with me and many times I've drawn upon it.

Just about every week these days, I see and hear about bullying and the act of it has been expanded to include threats from not just other students. It now includes teachers, neighbors, family members and even friends.

In addition, the definition has come to include not just physical violence, but also verbal and written threats and harassment. Plus, the penalties are expensive and time consuming. Win or lose, the problem is usually still there and seldom changes the behavior of the bully.

That young father is long gone, and so is that 11–year-old boy. But even as a grown man, I still reflect on memories and lessons learned from Dad. Among those many lessons one still stands out: He taught me how to stand up for myself and to win, even when I lost.

So, I'll take that night in Austin and my dad's advice not to run from adversity, but to meet it head on. That's when you learn, no matter your age, to "pony up" and "grow a pair."

Thanks again, Dad . . . for the "flagpole."

Jerry

The Thing in the Closet

by
Christine Cacciatore

I have a true obsession with scary things . . . the creepier, the better. I love Halloween, horror movies and thrillers. And I especially love scary books. As a teen, Steven King's *Pet Sematary* scared me so badly that at one point, I teared up and was physically unable to turn the page. I love stuff like that. That man has a gift, and that gift is to be able to "boo!" the stuffing right out of me.

I've always been this way. It started when I was a child, at an age that I was not even able to read yet. My mom and dad were very young parents. Just babies, really. Who really knows it all at 26? Certainly not the people masquerading as my parents.

So what would you do, as a parent, if your six-year-old daughter asked you to scare her? And when you told her, "No," said child pouted? Why, you would still tell her, "No." But if you were *my* parents, there would also be a calculating gleam in your eyes and a very bad, possibly *child-scarring* idea forming in the recesses of your mischievous parental brains.

And so it was, one Saturday afternoon, my dad was stretched out on the recliner, where dads are often found. I hopped up on his lap and snuggled next to him, in his white T-shirt, to watch TV for a while.

With no attention span to speak of, either then or now, I got bored almost immediately and went in search of my mother. I found her in the bathroom, standing in front of the mirror rubbing something black onto her eyes. She looked at me then said, with a grin on her face and a giggle in her voice, "Privacy, please. Go on. Go see your dad."

Ever obedient, I closed the door. *But why was she laughing?* I wondered. I then climbed back up into the recliner with Dad.

A short while later, Dad asked if I'd go into the hall closet and get his black uniform shoes. He was a police officer at the time, and this was a common request. He had to shine and polish his shoes all the time.

Innocently, I jumped off the chair and skipped over to the closet door, excited to be helping. I loved the smell of the black shoe polish.

What happened next is forever imprinted on my memory, as time seemed to stand still.

I opened the closet door, conveniently located across from Dad's chair. Immediately, a ghastly, child-eating creature loomed out over me with arms raised, emitting an unearthly, "*Bwaaaaaaa.*" The creature was all in white, with a horrid bumpy face and black holes where the eyes should be. That horrifying, menacing thing advanced on me and reached its arms out as if it were about to scoop me up and take me back into the closet where I'd be trapped forever.

I had seen enough, thank you very much. I whirled around, screaming, and ran as fast as I could back to my daddy. Even now, I am quite sure that my feet never touched the floor the whole way as I scurried from the closet to the recliner. My father has since confirmed this.

I monkeyed up into his lap, trembling and crying, and attempted to warn him against the hideous thing advancing on us when something occurred to me. He was laughing. He was laughing so hard he made a scratchy, wheezy sound. The recliner shook with the force of his amusement. Tears squirted out of his eyes and streamed down his face.

Startled at Dad's reaction, I was even more scared. Did he not realize the imminent danger we were in, with that terrible white devil coming closer?

Then, a second thing occurred in my fear-numbed brain. That white closet creature coming towards us could barely stand up because it, too, was laughing. Laughing *with Mom's laugh.* Apparently when I had interrupted my mother in the bathroom, she had been busily blacking out her eyes and putting shaving cream around her face, about to scare the snot out of her young daughter.

It all came together in my little kids' brain. I was *not* about to be eaten and dragged into the closet, never to be seen again. It was just my mom and dad playing a joke on me. Scaring me.

Like I had begged them to do, over and over.

Years later, I look back on that incident with adult eyes.

What were they thinking? How could they scar their child like that, ensuring years of therapy?

My warped sense of humor takes over, and I think, how could they NOT? They were only 26 years old. Young. No money. There were no "words with friends," computers or video games to occupy their time back then, just good, old-fashioned imagination. They sure put that to good use.

And in all fairness, I *had* asked. *Begged* them, after all. As good parents, they were merely doing what I had requested and in the process, made an unforgettable memory for us all.

You may think that after that episode, I shied away from anything scary ever again. That was not the case. In truth, it only whetted my appetite for more. That was a good thing, because my inventive, creative parents had plenty more tricks up their sleeves . . . and poor little me, at their mercy, to experience every one of them.

Christine

Rescuing Father

by
Marcia Byalick

In my father's 70th year, he lost his wife, moved to Florida, got remarried, gave up pastrami and began lifting weights seven days a week. In the 15 years since, he's nurtured friendships for the first time in my memory, incorporated running on the treadmill into his exercise routine and is presently midway through his second go-round as president of his condominium.

But now that he's 85, my sister and I began worrying about the work involved with his presidential position, including his fretting possibly that the details of last month's minutes, this week's elevator malfunction and today's estimates for a new roof were becoming too overwhelming. As sensitively as we could, we started encouraging him to resign.

We were grateful that decades of the wear and tear of 12-hour days, six days a week, spent sweating behind a pressing machine and inhaling insidious chemicals in his little dry cleaning store hadn't adversely affected his health. In fact, in his encore career as a retired man, he auditioned to be Hume Cronyn's stand-in for *Cocoon Two*, running back and forth on a basketball court. And he fought the U.S. Department of Housing and Urban Development when, a few months after 9/11, he refused to rent to a 27-year-old Saudi man on a student visa, saying *his* President told him to be vigilant. Although we were proud at how well he was taking care of himself, 85 was, after all, 85, and it was time for him to step down.

My sister and I decided to sweeten the deal by promising to fly to Florida whatever day the board met to hear his resignation. It wasn't easy for either of us—it was midweek at busy times in both our lives—but he needed his daughters. With the smugness that accompanies too many do-gooders, we left the responsibilities of home behind. We knew he was uneasy about how he would fill his time once he was no longer president, so we researched suggestions for volunteer jobs, collected brochures of places he might want to visit and created lists of movies he'd definitely enjoy. We brought enough hugs and smiles to cushion the transfer of power. Armed with all the current literature on how keeping the brain fed and interested will ensure it'll remain vigorous and resilient, we arrived to rescue our dad from the stressful overload of his board position.

The meeting began on the third floor of the condominium with the counting of ballots to determine who would be serving on the 2003 board. At the end of the night, my father would make his announcement. He refused our offer to help him compose a few sentences, along with our suggestion that he still serve on the board, but in a lesser capacity. We rolled our eyes, as our father—both feisty and stubborn—insisted he'd "wing it" when the time came.

There must have been 100 people waiting to hear the results. It was eye opening to absorb how the boundaries of old age were much broader and more diverse than we had pictured. Whether the result of luck or genes or financial security, there was little evidence in this group of the decline and dependency that often defines the elderly. In fact, if I were to be completely honest, there was probably a lot less sadness, nervousness and anxiety on display that night than at the professional meetings my sister and I regularly attended. While it's still true that old age is not for sissies, could it be that if you're fortunate enough to get there, you're actually happier?

The building manager announced the winners. My father smiled. I knew he was happy with the three new board members the building owners had chosen. Then he stood. My sister and I held hands. This was going to be hard for him to say.

"I'm so pleased with the makeup of our new board," our dad said in a strong voice. Then he grinned. "And I look forward to accomplishing great things together in the coming years."

He had to be kidding. He wasn't resigning. We had traveled 1,500 miles to be with him that night. And he didn't look the least bit sorry.

"Don't be mad," my sister whispered, "I'm relieved."

I sat in silence.

"If he messes up or finds it's too much for him, he'll resign then," she continued. "What makes us think we know better than he does what's best for him? We've never been old."

She was right, of course. Most of my bossy advice concerning growing older was a projection of my own fears and hopes. Why would they be more valid than what was before my eyes? If my dad were slower at remembering facts and acting on them, he was wiser at mulling, reflecting and arriving at confident decisions. Added to teaching me the importance of telling the truth, the hidden rewards in hard work and how to understand a basketball game, he had taught me one more valuable lesson: that you can teach a middle-aged dog new tricks. A happy, healthy old age lies not in the stars . . . or in our children's advice . . . but in ourselves.

Marcia's father, Al, and her daughter
Jennifer at Jennifer's wedding in 2006

NYMB Series Founders

Together, Dahlynn and Ken McKowen have 60-plus years of professional writing, editing, publication, marketing and public relations experience. Full-time authors and travel writers, the two have such a large body of freelance work that when they reached more than 2,000 articles, stories and photographs published, they stopped counting. And the McKowens are well respected ghostwriters, having worked with CEOs and founders of some of the nation's biggest companies. They have even ghostwritten for a former U.S. president and a few California governors and elected officials.

From 1999 to 2009, Ken and Dahlynn were consultants and coauthors for *Chicken Soup for the Soul,* where they collaborated with series founders Jack Canfield and Mark Victor Hansen on several books such as *Chicken Soup for the Entrepreneur's Soul; Chicken Soup for the Soul in Menopause; Chicken Soup for the Fisherman's Soul;* and *Chicken Soup for the Soul: Celebrating Brothers and Sisters.* They also edited and ghost-created many more Chicken titles during their tenure, with Dahlynn reading more than 100,000 story submissions.

For highly acclaimed outdoor publisher Wilderness Press, the McKowens' books include *Best of Oregon and Washington's Mansions, Museums and More; The Wine-Oh! Guide to California's Sierra Foothills* and national award-winning *Best of California's Missions, Mansions and Museums.*

Under Publishing Syndicate, the couple authored and

published *Wine Wherever: In California's Mid-Coast & Inland Region*, and are actively researching wineries for *Wine Wherever: In California's Paso Robles Region*, the second book in the Wine Wherever series.

If that's not enough, the McKowens are also the creators of the Wine Wherever iPhone mobile winery-destination journaling app and are currently creating a travel television show under the same brand (www.WineWherever.com).

Ken with son Jason

Ten-year-old Shawn with Mom (Dahlynn)

NYMB Co-Creator

About Pat Nelson

Pat Nelson was an afterthought, a surprise to her parents, Lee and Ella Hedglin, who already had two teenage sons.

"Patty" was born in Bemidji, Minnesota. There was no hospital in her tiny hometown of Puposky. Her brothers had been delivered at home by Dr. Mary Ghostley, superintendent of the Lake Julia Tuberculosis Sanatorium, where their parents worked.

During her early years, Patty lived on the sanatorium property at the Lake Julia San Dairy, which her father operated. Even though she left Puposky at age four, she never forgot her roots and is writing a book titled *Open Window* about "The San," its patients and its progressive lady doctor.

When she was five, Pat moved with her family to Longview, Washington. She lived there for many years and graduated from R. A. Long High School and Lower Columbia College. Pat is a member of Willamette Writers, Portland, Oregon. She attends Write Your Life Story and WordFest in Longview and Cedar Creek Writers in Amboy, Washington. She learned to love the written word and particularly enjoyed creating humor through word play. That is often evident in her writing today.

Pat worked for IPCO Federal Credit Union in Longview for several years and wrote the book *You . . . The Credit Union Member*. She writes columns for *The Valley Bugler*, Longview,

Washington, and has written columns for *The Daily News*, Longview. She contributes stories to www.lewisriver.com. Her stories have also appeared in *Chicken Soup for the Soul* and *Not Your Mother's Book . . . On Being a Woman; On Being a Stupid Kid; On Dogs; On Travel* and now in *On Being a Parent*, which she co-created. She is also co-creating *NYMB . . . On Being a Grandparent* and *On Working for a Living*. Both books are still accepting story submissions. She blogs at www.storystorm.me. Pat is available to speak to groups in her area about the *Not Your Mother's Books* series.

Pat lives on a small lake in Woodland, Washington with her husband, Bob, a Great Dane and Labradoodle mix named Brisa, and a Manx cat named Peso. She has had careers in credit union marketing, in restaurant ownership, in retail and in wholesale, but she says parenting her two kids, Steve and Susan, was the best job of all.

Pat at her local bookstore

Contributor Bios

Jerry Baker is a native Texan residing in Plano, Texas with his wife Kathy and the fur pack: Hank, Samantha and Abby. His alma mater is Texas Tech University. After college, Jerry proudly served in the U.S. Marine Corps before starting a life-long career in the life insurance industry.

Kathleene S. Baker and husband Jerry live in Plano, Texas. An avid dog lover, Kathleene is the co-creator of *Not Your Mother's Book...On Dogs* and the upcoming *Not Your Mother's Book...On Pets*. She has contributed to numerous publications and anthologies and writes three columns.

Cynthia Ballard Borris is the author of *No More Bobs* and is an award-winning writer. A humor columnist, she is a former board member of the National Society of Newspaper Columnists and is a frequent contributor to *Chicken Soup for the Soul* and other publications. Contact: cynthiaborris@gmail.com or cynthiaborris.blogspot.com

Pam Bostwick, who is hearing and visually impaired, has had many articles published in magazines, newspapers and anthologies. She enjoys her condo and its peaceful, sunny surroundings, but misses the beach. Pam performs with her guitar, mentors others and adores seven children and 17 grandchildren. She happily remarried on 7/7/07. Email: pamloves7@comcast.net

Debra Ayers Brown is Meredith's mom and a writer, humorist, blogger, magazine columnist and award-winning marketing professional. Her stories have appeared in *Guideposts, Chicken Soup for the Soul, Woman's World, Liberty Life* and others. She is a Southeastern Writers Association board member. Connect with her at www.About.Me/DebraAyersBrown or visit www.DebraAyersBrown.com.

James Butler has been writing for 30 years. His work has been published in hobby and trade magazines, science fiction and children's adventure books, newsletters and in *NYMB...On Being a Stupid Kid*. He won the Alumni Student Writing Award at Walsh College, in Troy, Michigan. Visit Jim at www.Facebook.com/RaptorRavine.

Marcia Byalick is a young-adult novelist, a columnist for several Long Island publications, a frequent contributor to *The New York Times* and *Newsday* and a teacher of memoir writing. She loves sharing the stories of her life and hopes to encourage others to do the same.

Christine Cacciatore is married to a wonderful man, has three great kids, a new granddaughter and one ridiculous dog. She and her sister Jennifer Starkman co-wrote and recently published *Baylyn, Bewitched,* the first book in *The Whitfield Witch Series,* available now as an e-book on Amazon, Barnes & Noble and Smashwords.

Kathe Campbell lives her dream on a Montana mountain with her mammoth donkeys, a Keeshond and kitties. Three children, 11 grandkids and four greats round out her herd. She writes on Alzheimer's and is a contributing author to *Chicken Soup for the Soul* and the *Not Your Mother's Book* anthology series.

David Carkeet's novels include a trilogy with a linguist as the unlikely hero— *Double Negative, The Full Catastrophe* and *The Error of Our Ways.* His essays have appeared in The New York Times Magazine, *The Village Voice, Smithsonian* and *Poets & Writers.* He lives in Vermont.

Liane Kupferberg Carter is a journalist whose articles and essays have appeared in many publications, including *The New York Times,* the *Chicago Tribune* and the *Huffington Post.*

Dawn Caunce, a United Kingdom-based writer, is a busy mum of three. Her short stories appear in *NYMB...On Being a Stupid Kid* and other anthologies. In her spare time, Dawn moderates on an international writing forum and is currently working on a middle-grade children's book.

Kari Lynn Collins is a humor columnist and advertising director at the *Iowa Park Leader,* a weekly newspaper in Texas, and blogs at www.karilynncollins.com. She is also a wife, mother and seeker of fun!

Shari Courter has been married to her husband, Ron, for 20 years. They have one son, Zac, and three daughters—Aubrey, Kearstin and Caymen. Shari is a stay-at-home mom and a licensed massage therapist. In her spare time, she enjoys blogging about her family's antics.

Zona Crabtree graduated from Texas Woman's University. While teaching speech and English, she met her husband, Joe, and traded teaching for farming. She is a member of the Ozark Writers League and the Western Writers of America. She and her family live in southwestern Missouri.

Kathryn Cureton writes from the basement lair of her backwoods mansion, eight-tenths of a mile up a gravel road in southeast Missouri. She makes her living teaching physics and biology to high school students who are not all that impressed with her status as a former high school valedictorian.

Ellen Denton is a freelance writer living in the Rocky Mountains with her husband and two demonic cats. She has been published in various magazines and anthologies, both fiction and non-fiction. This is her third story in the *Not Your Mother's Book* anthology series.

Elizabeth Deroshia lives in Athens, Georgia with her muse, Justice, now 12. Earning her English degree from UGA spoiled her for work in the "real world," so she continues to pursue freelance writing jobs, higher education and spending time with her extended family, a constant source of comical writing material.

Klazina Dobbe, with her husband and three children, immigrated to the U.S. from the Netherlands in 1980 and started the Holland America Bulb Farm. Klazina became interested in alternative healing and earned a master's degree in acupuncture and Oriental medicine. She is currently writing a book based on her experiences.

Charles Dowdy is a broadcaster and writer living in Louisiana with his wife and four children. His website is CharlesWDowdy.com.

Norine Dworkin-McDaniel is the creator of the humor blogs *Science of Parenthood* and *Don't Put Lizards in Your Ears*. She writes for many national magazines and websites, including *More, Health, Parents, All You, Marie Claire, Redbook, American Baby, iVillage* and *Lifescript*.

Terri Elders lives near Colville, Washington. A lifelong writer and editor, her stories have appeared in dozens of periodicals and anthologies. She is the co-creator for *Not Your Mother's Book...On Travel*. She blogs at atouchoftarragon.blogspot. com. Terri is a public member of the Washington State Medical Quality Assurance Commission.

Carole Fowkes is the author of six books published by Ink Lion Books. Her articles and stories have appeared in anthologies, including her story "Up a Tree" in *Not Your Mother's Book...On Being a Stupid Kid*. She currently lives in Dallas, Texas.

Virginia Funk has had stories published in *Omni News* and *Chicken Soup for the Soul*. Her love of books inspired her to attend creative writing classes at her community college. This is her first story in the *Not Your Mother's Book* series.

Catherine Giordano is a public speaker, writer, blogger and poet living in Orlando, Florida. Her books include *The Poetry Connection, What Ifs, If Only, So Whets* and *News Print Poetry 2012*. Her stories and poetry have been published in several magazines and anthologies. Catherine's website is www.talksallabout.com.

T'Mara Goodsell is a multi-genre writer and teacher who lives near St. Louis, Missouri. She has written for *Chicken Soup for the Soul*, as well as various other anthologies, newspapers and publications. She has two young adult children who make life's adventure sweeter than rocky road ice cream.

Stacey Gustafson has a humor column called "Are You Kidding Me?" based on her suburban family and everyday life. Her stories have appeared in *Chicken Soup for the Soul: The Magic of Mothers and Daughters* and *Not Your Mother's Book...On Being a Woman*. Check out her blog at www.staceygustafson.com, Twitter @mepaint.

Stacey Hatton, pediatric nurse, mom and humorist, always investigates the "funny bone." Her humor column appears in the *Kansas City Star*, an essay appears in *My Funny Major Medical* and *I Just Want to Pee Alone*. Stacey received the "2012 Circle of Moms Top 25 Book Author Moms award." Blog: www.nursemommylaughs.com

Nancy Hershorin grew up in Fresno, California, where she raised three daughters. She has traveled extensively and lived for several years in Western Australia. Nancy loves to cook and enjoys writing amusing stories about her life. Now retired, she lives in Eugene, Oregon to be close to her three-year-old granddaughter.

Erika Hoffman raised four kids, taught hundreds of others, and now writes inspirational essays, humorous stories and occasionally a mystery.

Lucy James writes from the rolling foothills of the Appalachian Mountains in eastern Kentucky. Her short stories and poetry have previously appeared in *The Citron Review*, *A Generation Defining Itself: Vol. 8*, *The Truth Magazine* and *Gemini Magazine*.

Sarah L. Johnson lives in Canada where she reads, writes, runs and occasionally overuses the word "perpendicular."

Ashley Jones lives in Frisco, Texas with her husband, David, and her children Garrett and Lyla. She's a former special education teacher turned stay-at-home mommy-blogger. Ashley loves sharing her funniest—and most embarrassing—parenting moments with others. Follow Ashley's blog at www.becominglucy.com.

Janet Sheppard Kelleher is a Southern columnist who laughs when people ask, "How do you get funny ideas?" She says, "Wit happens! All I have to do is describe it!" Her books *Big C, Little Ta-Tas* and *Havin' My Cotton-Pickin' Say* should debut this year or next.

Lisa McManus Lange gazes at the moon, looking for cooking inspiration. Multi-published by *Chicken Soup for the Soul* and Publishing Syndicate, Lisa also blogs at www.lisamcmanuslange.blogspot.com. She can be reached at lisamc2010@yahoo.ca.

Mary Laufer is a freelance writer and substitute teacher in Saint Cloud, Florida. Her essays, short stories and poems have been published in magazines, newspapers and several anthologies.

John J. Lesjack, a graduate of East Detroit High School and San Francisco State College, is an active freelance writer. His works have appeared in *Instructor, Science of Mind, The Ultimate Mom, Chicken Soup for the Soul* and *Not Your Mother's Book...On Being a Stupid Kid.*

Connie Lissner is a writer, lawyer, wife and, most importantly, the mother of two boys. She navigates the slippery slope of motherhood one day at a time and blogs to tell about it at www.isuckasaparent.com.

Linda A. Lohman, BA, RHS, QMB, LOL, has short stories or contributions in *Chicken Soup for the Soul, NYMB* and *Miss Kitty's Journal*. Writing from Sacramento, California, she thanks editors and critique groups for pushing her sled. She also thanks her family for providing unlimited material. Reach her at lindaalohman@yahoo.com.

Mary Beth Magee managed to survive parenting her little grouch and now enjoys the delightfulness of her terrific adult son and his lovely wife. She's just waiting for them to become parents and experience a little payback! Meanwhile, she's back in touch with her Southern roots and loving it.

David Martin's humor and political satire have appeared in many publications including *The New York Times,* the *Chicago Tribune* and *Smithsonian Magazine*. His latest humor collection, *Screams & Whispers,* is available on Amazon.com. David lives in Ottawa, Canada with his wife, Cheryl, and their daughter Sarah.

Timothy Martin is the author of *Rez Rock, There's Nothing Funny About Running, Summer With Dad* and *Wimps Like Me.* He has two novels due out in 2013: *Fast Pitch* (Cedar Grove Books) and *Somewhere Down The Line* (Neverland Publishing). Tim has done commentary on National Public Radio.

Laurel (Bernier) McHargue was raised as "Daughter #4" of five girls in Braintree, Massachusetts where she lived until heading to Smith College, followed by the United States Military Academy. Her constant quest for adventure landed her in Leadville, Colorado where she currently resides with her husband. Read more at www.leadvillelaurel.com.

Kimberly McRaney-Blake—busy wife and mother of two teenage boys—works at least two, sometimes three, jobs, but still finds time to host barbecues and birthday parties at her home and go camping with family and friends. This is her first published story.

Carole Ann Moleti works as a nurse-midwife in New York City. Her fiction and nonfiction focuses on women's and political issues. This essay is the intro to her mommy memoir *Karma, Kickbacks and Kids*. Her work has appeared in a variety of literary venues including *NYMB...On Being a Woman*.

Karen Mykietka is a mother of two living in Edmonton, Alberta, Canada. After many years of university, she explored qualitative health research, midwifery advocacy and writing. She next undertook homeschooling and community development. She continues to work on a variety of community projects while running a community newspaper.

Wendy Nelson lives in Ontario, Canada with her husband and two boys. When she's not busy being a hockey mom, you can find her, notebook in hand, writing short stories and dark thrillers. See Wendy's other contribution to the NYMB series in *NYMB...On Being a Woman*.

Rose Ella Putnam, at 92 years old, has raised three children and outlived her husband of 59-and-a-half years. Rose plays pinochle and cribbage, attends a Write Your Life Story group and tried Haiku for the first time, winning a contest in her age bracket. She has many stories to tell.

Cappy Hall Rearick is a syndicated newspaper columnist, an award-winning short story writer and the author of six books and five successful columns. Featured by Erma Bombeck Writers' Workshop as a Humor Writer of the Month, Rearick's humor and short fiction has been read and enjoyed in anthologies throughout the country.

Betty J. Roan has written over 100 short stories, several of which have been published in a book titled *The Apple Tree*. She is currently working on a tween series titled *The Dirt Foot Gang*. She resides in Toledo, Illinois with her husband, Robert.

Kendall Roderick's stomach still turns when she smells diesel, but at least she has gotten better at throwing a stick. She continues to write daily, while still leaving time to enjoy her wonderful husband and play with her three furry children.

Maureen Rogers is a transplanted Canadian living in Seattle, Washington. Her writing projects include fiction, poetry and essays. She has been published online, in newspapers and in several anthologies. Her current project, *Hose Jockeys, Hotshots and Heroes*, is a collection based on the careers of urban firefighters. Contact: morogers@gmail.com

Susan Rose is currently writing a young adult novel, Legends of the Deep. She is a mother of two and enjoys creating "upcycled" art from magazines. Her artwork is displayed in homes and galleries across the United States.

Julie Royce, attorney, is currently editing her historical fiction story *Ardent Spirit*, about American fur trader Magdelaine LaFramboise. She recently published *PILZ,* a crime thriller, and is working on a sequel. Julie has published two travel guides and writes a monthly travel column for www.wanderingeducators.com. Her website and blog are at www.jkroyce.com.

Stephen Rusiniak is a husband and father from Wayne, New Jersey. As a former police detective, he specialized in and lectured on juvenile/family matters, but now shares his thoughts through his writings. His work has appeared in various publications and book anthologies. Contact: stephenrusiniak@yahoo.com or visit www.Facebook.com/StephenPRusiniak.

Elizabeth Sandahl enjoys a busy life. She started writing stories about her life four years ago and enjoys sharing her life experiences with family and friends. Elizabeth likes to add humor to her stories, saying, "Life is funny!" This is her first story in the *Not Your Mother's Book* series.

Donna Collins Tinsley, wife, mother and grandmother, lives in Port Orange, Florida and has been included in several magazines and book compilations. Her subjects range from wacky hormones to healing from sexual abuse. For information or to join Somebody's Mother Online Prayer Support Group, email Thornrose7@aol.com.

Lisa Tognola shares her views on everything from marriage to morals to mistresses. This Jersey girl highlights the humorous side of suburban life: the good, the bad and the ugly in her blog http://mainstreetmusingsblog.com/. She contributes to the American humor newspaper *Funny Times* and online magazine *More.com.* Twitter @lisatognola

Pearl Vork-Zambory blogs at pearl-whyyoulittle.blogspot.com on commuting via the city bus, corporate cubicle-ism, the abusive nature of her cats, and, infrequently, her laundry. She has read and spoken at Metro State University in Minneapolis, Minnesota where her chapbook *I was Raised to be a Lert* has been used as a textbook.

Ernie Witham writes the nationally-syndicated column "Ernie's World" for the *Montecito Journal* in Santa Barbara, California. He is the author of two humor books and leads humor writing workshops at several conferences. He has been published in many anthologies, including *NYMB...On Travel.*

Pam Young is co-author of *Sidetracked Home Executives: From Pigpen to Paradise*, selling more than a million and a half copies. Today, Pam shares her humor and wisdom on www.makeitfunanditwillgetdone.com with a daily video for homemakers of all ages. Her motto is: Make it fun and it will get done!

Story Permissions

The Flagpole © 2012 Jerry W. Baker
Just Call Me Gypsy © 2012 Kathleene S. Baker
It's How You Play the Game © 2007 Cynthia Borris
Double the Fun © 2006 Pamela Bostwick
The Ups and Downs of Shopping © 2012 Debra Ayers Brown
The Big Sale © 2012 James L. Butler
Rescuing Father © 2010 Marcia Byalick
The Thing in the Closet © 2012 Christine Cacciatore
Huckleberry Hounds © 2011 Kathleen M. Campbell
Field Notes from the Playroom Floor © 2003 David Carkeet
When Mom "Likes" Too Much © 2011 Liane Kupferberg Carter
The Modest Mom © 2012 Dawn Keeley Caunce
The Pussy Riot © 2012 Kari Lynn Collins
Parenting 911 © 2003 Lorie Conley
The Family Photo © 2010 Shari Courter
A Tale of a Tail © 2012 Zona Mae Crabtree
Cheese Cutting 101 © 2012 Kathryn Cureton
The Trip © 2011 Ellen Denton
Get Your Ass Off My Patio! © 2005 Elizabeth Ashley Deroshia
If Only He Were a Leg Man © 2005 Elizabeth Ashley Deroshia
Throwing in the Towel © 2013 Klazina Dobbe
Will Pee for M&M's © 2012 Charles W. Dowdy Jr.
Hanging 'Round the Men's Room © 2010 Norine Dworkin-McDaniel
In Tune with My Son © 2010 Theresa J. Elders
The Fountain of Youth © 2010 Betty Enigk
Musically Gifted © 2012 Carole Fowkes
The "Baby" Bottle © 2012 Virginia M. Funk
Figuring It Out © 2012 Catherine Giordano
The Rocky Road of Parenthood © 2011 T'Mara Goodsell
Mr. Know-It-All © 2013 Stacey Gustafson
Smarter Than the Average Bear © 2012 Stacey Hatton
Nobody Likes Me © 2012 Nancy Caldwell Hershorin
Hooked Up © 2010 Erika V. Hoffman
World War IV © 2012 Sarah Johnson

Publishing Syndicate

Publishing Syndicate LLC is an independent book publisher based in Northern California. The company has been in business for more than a decade, mainly providing writing, ghostwriting and editing services for major publishers. In 2011, Publishing Syndicate took the next step and expanded into a full-service publishing house.

The company is owned by married couple Dahlynn and Ken McKowen. Dahlynn is the CEO and publisher, and Ken serves as president and managing editor.

Publishing Syndicate's mission is to help writers and authors realize personal success in the publishing industry, and, at the same time, provide an entertaining reading experience for its customers. From hands-on book consultation and their very popular and free monthly *Wow Principles* publishing tips e-newsletter to forging book deals with both new and experienced authors and launching three new anthology series, Publishing Syndicate has created a powerful and enriching environment for those who want to share their writing with the world. (www.PublishingSyndicate.com)

NYMB Needs Your Stories!

We are looking for hip, fun, modern and very-much-today type stories, just like those in this book, for 30 new titles in the *NYMB* series. Published contributors are compensated.

Submission guidelines at www.PublishingSyndicate.com

317

More *NYMB* Titles

Look for new
Not Your Mother's Books
coming soon!